Moo...

The Salmon

Fi...le

Mooching

The Salmon Fisherman's Bible

hancock

house

by David Nuttall

ISBN 0-88839-072-6
Copyright © 1980 David Nuttall

Cataloging in Publication Data

Nuttall, David, 1934-
  Mooching for Salmon

  ISBN 0-88839-072-6
  1. Salmon Fishing. I. Title. II. Series.
SH685.N88   799.1'755   C80-091188-1

Typesetting Janet Miller, Dana Cleland
*Production*Pulp Press

799.1

Distributed in the United States by
Universe Books, 381 Park Avenue South, New York, 10016
Tel (212) 685-7400

Published by
HANCOCK HOUSE PUBLISHERS LTD.
#10 Orwell Street, North Vancouver, B.C. Canada V7J 3K1

Contents

1 Definition and History 9

2 Some General Principles 17

3 Let's Tackle Up 27

4 The Moocher's Knot And How To Tie It 41

5 Safety And Courtesy Ashore And
   On The Water 55

6 Birds And Herring And Things 63

7 Chinook And Coho 77

8 Feeding Habits: Coho Vs. Chinook 87

9 Mooching Techniques Generally 101

10 Troll-Mooching 111

11 Some Of The Finer Points...................... 119

12 The Fish You Will Catch And
    How To Handle Them 133

13 Care And Cleaning............................. 145

14 How To Build Your Own Rod 169

Foreword

I have pursued both the Mighty Chinook (Spring) and the Scrappy Coho (Silver) salmon all along the Pacific Coast of North America since the late 1930s. In 1952 under the instruction of the late Lt. Col. W.E. "Squid" MacInnes, my tactics changed from trolling to light-tackle fishing, exclusively strip casting and mooching.

Since then, I have fished in the company of, as well as alongside, many of the truly ardent and highly successful moochers of the British Columbia coast. I have learned much from each of them. I include Ray McCormick, Gord Bush, Dennis Angelussi, Don Younie, Lee Straight, the late "Colly" Peacock, Bernie Hanby, Vic Faulkes, Sam Anderson, Earl Anderson, Mike Cramond, Lloyd Stewart, George Nash and Len Larson.

When David Hancock, this book's publisher, asked me to review Mr. Nuttall's manuscript for accuracy of techniques and general information value, I was delighted at the opportunity.

What you will find contained in the pages of this book, will inform, educate and entertain you. Mr. Nuttall has not only given a complete and accurate description of the techniques and skills required to become a highly successful moocher, but also — and to my mind this is far more important — has eloquently transmitted the big picture. The experiences, situations and feelings that can happen to you while fishing our waters come across very vividly.

Mr. Nuttall's obvious respect for the salmon themselves, and the need for conservation and enhancement is clearly demonstrated as well. His observations and anecdotes concerning all the other creatures of the sea, both wild and domestic, will bring smiles to all who read them.

I recommend this book, *Mooching: The Salmon Fisherman's Bible,* to you most highly and most sincerely. Nowhere else could you find such a complete treatise on the sport and esthetic experience of light-tackle fishing for salmon.

Ted Peck
West Vancouver
1980

1

Definition And History

Mooching for salmon is increasing in popularity and will continue to do so because it is an engagement which utterly captivates the participant. Most people enjoy fishing, have tried fishing, but have given it up because the success factor has not been there. Mooching is not a guarantee of success so much as a balancing factor which makes success probable. Coupled with the improved chances of success are a variety of side benefits which make mooching much more attractive than trolling.

Not least among these is the pleasure of playing your fish with nothing between you and it but a two-ounce weight. No dodger, no planer, no cumbersome sixteen-ounce weight; just you and the fish. It makes quite a difference.

Mooching is a personal sport. You have to watch your rod tip carefully, then apply yourself to the little techniques necessary to hook the salmon when that rod tip has signalled the presence of the fish. Although many salmon will hook themselves, the experienced moocher can greatly improve his chances of success by applying himself to the sport - or herself as the case may be, for it is one of the few sports where women are on an equal footing with any man. Because mooching requires a minimum of muscle and a maximum of concentration and skill, it is attracting more and more women. Anyone can learn the basic techniques, and once mastered it then becomes a matter of adding to your fund of knowledge, using a little intuition and having a little luck!

The basic mooching techniques will put fish in boats, but because mooching is a highly developed art with such a variety of tricks and techniques, it lends itself to serious competition.

Mooching at its best is an art; a delicate, sensitive and highly developed art requiring substantial skill and knowledge. Moochers therefore tend to become, at least to some extent, competitive. Seldom will a moocher reveal the finer points of the art and almost never will he share his entire fund of knowledge with anyone. Each moocher has certain tricks of the art that he keeps to himself to give him that fine edge which will put a fish on his table while others have none.

Without any doubt, it is a more effective method of fishing than trolling. An added bonus is the fact that mooching, in the main, is carried on without the boat motor running, so the silence of the sport adds to the beauty of it.

Experts such as Lee Straight, Ted Peck and Mike Crammond have popularized mooching by engaging very successfully in the sport and writing of their successes and their techniques. Anyone who has read Lee Straight's beautiful story on Chinook in Jack Grundle's *British Columbia Game Fish,* published in 1970, will appreciate the magnificence of the sport. Similarly, Ted Peck and Mike Cramond have done much to increase its popularity. All three men are excellent fishermen and inveterate moochers.

There are others who have earned for themselves reputations as "moochers": the Sewells, Ollie Morrison, Ray McCormick, Jo-Jo McMeekan, John Schleimer, Chuck Jones, Al Christie, and Al Davidson, the sportscaster, are all men of skill and tenacity who have earned reputations along our coast. There are others, too, who excel at the sport, but are not known as well. Moochers are generally proud of their skill and will cheerfully take a salmon out from under your nose when you are catching none and enjoy to the fullest extent the puzzled look on your face.

Despite the many excellent articles and one or two short books published on mooching, there has not been any serious attempt to qualify the definition of the term "mooching" nor any serious attempt to explain many of the finer points.

There are many reasons for this. Our fund of knowledge touching Pacific salmon is growing rapidly. Almost as soon as an article is written, the material is, in good part, outdated, having been improved upon or discovered to be in error. The writing of a definitive book on mooching is therefore a formidable task.

Some of what lies between these covers has been said before; some of the ideas or theories will be proven to be wrong; yet there exists the need for a comprehensive book, a gathering of knowledge with the object of sharing that knowledge. This book is not, however, simply a gathering of knowledge. It is an invitation to fishermen and to those who will become fishermen to explore the ideas set forth here; many are entirely original and based upon personal observation; some have been gleaned from literature on the subject while others have been adopted from opinions gathered and later confirmed or modified. Nevertheless, the writer is not a biologist or a zoologist, hence suffers (or perhaps benefits) from a lack of rigid scientific training. As well, circumstances have not always allowed the fullest testing of the theories propounded.

Mooching is a form of still fishing involving a fairly long rod with a sensitive tip, a simple reel without any gears or bales called a "single-action" reel, light test line and either a herring strip or a live herring for bait. The weight is a simple crescent weight of one and one-half or two ounces. The basic knots, save one, are simple but in any event the leaders can be purchased ready made. The herring strip or live herring is attached to the leader by two small hooks and the bait is then lowered either to just above the bottom or to a depth, say fifty feet, which is thought to be promising. The rod tip is then watched for the "mooch." The trick is that the salmon frequently mouth the bait but don't swallow it, so the fish must be struck at just the right moment. Learning to read the rod tip is a big part of it. Next comes the actual playing of the fish.

The bait being such a universal food, the quarry may be quite a surprise for although it may be a salmon, it could be a huge lingcod, or a rockfish, dogfish, boccacio, red snapper or even a squid. Mooching is a great way to fish for cod so if you are not doing so well salmon fishing, you can always cuddle up to the shore to catch a few cod, always a treat to eat.

The playing of the fish will depend, of course, on what type of fish you have hooked. Most bottom fish come to the surface easily with the exception of the larger lingcod. These must be brought in very slowly. With care you can land a fifty-pound ling on fifteen-pound test line. Almost any salmon will engage your complete attention for at least ten minutes, the really big ones for an hour or more.

The use of the word "mooching" probably arises from the original dictionary meaning which is to amble, saunter, or wander aimlessly. This, of course, describes the basic technique which is to fish from a boat which is not under power. It is, in effect, a form of still fishing or "nigger fishing" as our southern neighbors sometimes say. The second meaning given by the dictionary is "to cadge or steal - to take without giving." This fits nicely in the context in which the word is used because that is precisely what the Chinook is trying to do down at the other end of the line. My lifelong friend Peter Broomhall used to say that sometimes there is a jerk on each end of the line! Of course the word has acquired different connotations and meanings in different areas here along the west coast of British Columbia and down into the United States. As with any sport there are variations of technique which lend themselves to the art of mooching which, while not mooching in the strict sense of the word, fall within the general term by reason of their similarity in technique and the use of the same terminal tackle.

There exists a problem as to just what techniques to include in the general term "mooching." There are some mooching techniques that involve trolling, which make any clear-cut definition somewhat difficult. It is necessary to examine in some detail the history of mooching and related techniques.

Inquiries indicate that mooching probably started as a result of alert strip-casters noting that salmon would frequently take a herring strip that was just dangling in the water, being neither trolled nor cast. It can be readily understood that a man strip-casting would occasionally leave his baits dangling in the water either when interrupted in his casting to attend to something else or perhaps just leaving it there while having a sandwich.

Earl Anderson, who has been an ardent sports fisherman all his long life, says he first learned the basic technique from an American gardener he met while they were employed building a miniature golf course late in the nineteen twenties. Earl was at that time an enthusiastic sports troller fisherman out of Vancouver's Horseshoe Bay. The American chap he met was having great success using a light weight and herring strip off nearby Point Atkinson. Earl gave it a try and in time showed others. As far as he can recall this was somewhere around 1929. To his knowledge only he and his friends were using this method. He says Dan Sewell, Sr., Lee Shaner, Bill Bertram and a man named Lammar all worked at developing the system. Most used a single hook through the top of the herring strip and let the second hook, a triple barbed one, just dangle alongside the strip.

Lee Straight, who is a man of great reliability and knowledge, puts the date at least ten years later - in and around 1940 through to 1945. He says Danny Sewell, Sr. learned the technique from Americans who were here sports fishing at the beginning of the war. It was called "nigger fishing" and practiced by men who were more often than not "cut spinning" — fishing with strips of herring cut at just the right angle to produce a slow roll of the strip. Lee recalls the word "mooch" came into being first in the San Francisco area. Here they were using heavy drop weights to take the strip down below the warm water thermals to the cold layer and moving their boats very slowly, so slowly as to be barely moving. The word "mooch" seemed to fit that particular action. At Rivers Inlet, the technique of fishing using heavy weight and slow movement involves the use of a four-ounce weight, a leader of six to ten feet, two single 2/0 Eagle Claw hooks tied in tandem and a plug-cut herring, cut so as to roll over slowly in the current and/or with the motion of the boat.

Lee Straight's explanation seems very sensible when you consider the proportionately higher number of Americans who fish Rivers Inlet. They probably brought with them the same techniques they used on their own coast.

Inquiries around San Francisco and Monterey today indicate the slow-troll plug-cut method is still in vogue and still producing a fair number of Chinooks. A very high percentage of sports fishermen at the docks in this area use the cut spinning technique Lee Straight describes, sometimes putting a small spinner in front of it and nearly always with light weight and about an eight-foot leader. The strip, if trolled behind the boat without a spinner, is biased on the front to produce a roll and is trolled at a fairly high speed in the wake of the boat as a method of catching Coho.

Americans generally, as salt-water fishermen, lean heavily to the plug-cut system, trolling it very slowly with weights from two ounces right up to six ounces and often as far down as ninety or even one hundred and twenty feet although when trolled behind the boat, the usual length of line out is somewhere between forty and eighty feet.

Given that type of fisherman and a man who is tired of rowing or who stops to play a fish on one rod leaving the other bait in the water, it is reasonable to assume that mooching would develop as a separate fishing technique.

We find then that the plug-cut troller is now using a new technique. He is stopping the motion of the boat and allowing his plug-cut to simply sit in the water. He holds the boat against the current or moves it very slowly and allows the plug-cut to work in the current or the motion of the boat to give it some movement.

It seems, therefore, highly likely that mooching emanated as an off-shoot of plug-cut trolling and/or spin trolling and/or strip-casting. All three of these techniques involve a rapidly moving bait, but each of the techniques would involve the incidental leaving of bait still in the water. Whether or not one would wish to give any particular one of these three techniques the edge in having developed mooching is very difficult to say. It could be strenuously argued that the very slow trolling of a plug-cut herring was probably the birth of the mooching technique but the answer probably lies in the simple proposition that the sport of mooching developed as an off-shoot of all three techniques.

Those who strip-cast with any regularity will tell you that it is very definitely wise to leave one herring strip over the side of the boat about twenty feet down to catch those fish which follow in the stripped bait and then give up the quest just before the strip reaches the surface. These salmon frequently make a turn away from the stripped bait and will take the strip that is just sitting still in the water. No doubt this technique was discovered early by strip-casters. There is a strip-casting technique mentioned later in this book which involves the simple dropping of the strip slowly down from the surface of the water, which method is very definitely a mooching technique, and very effective.

It seems sensible to include in any discussion of mooching the related systems of salmon fishing which use the same terminal tackle, namely trolling plug-cut herring or strip without a dodger and whether it be in the immediate wake (as in buck-tailing with a buck-tail fly) or far behind the boat, and whether it be a fast troll (as in buck-tailing) or a dead slow movement with heavy weight keeping the bait almost directly beneath the boat. It is all mooching, really, because of the terminal tackle. There are those who will argue that the boat in mooching can never be under power, but this must be fallacious. Otherwise, how are we to distinguish between a slowly rowed boat and one which is moving more quickly?

Unfortunately, in British Columbia the term "mooch" has become restricted. The meaning is often taken to cover little more than still fishing. The term should not be restricted. The term "power mooch" has come into being to cover the "trolling" of a light weight and herring and perhaps this terminology has some merit to distinguish between still fishing and trolling the same bait. Whether or not still fishing with a heavy weight and a spoon but no dodger, as practiced in some areas, particularly Campbell River and Rivers Inlet, is mooching is a somewhat more difficult question. The answer is probably that it is most definitely mooching because the fisherman, while not offering a · bait, is offering something that is intended to look like a bait and most important of all there is no dodger. The presence or absence of a dodger seems to be an important difference in defining the term "mooching."

A downrigger trolling a single line with a live herring or strip, which is the proper terminal tackle for mooching, should definitely *not* qualify as mooching because, while the dodger may not be present, the tackle is designed to be used only while moving; to be a true mooching technique, the use of the tackle must favor still fishing, that is it must be capable of that use.

If for instance, as often happens, you are mooching but decide to move to a different spot and you leave your tackle in the water as you move and take a salmon right on the surface, the bait really being trolled as you move over to the new spot, are you then to be said to have caught the fish while trolling? You came out to mooch, you were initially mooching, you caught the fish on mooching bait, and you caught it at a time when you intended to continue mooching with the same tackle that you started with. It seems fair to say that you caught the fish while mooching.

The two distinguishing features of mooching should be that there be no dodger or flasher and the tackle must be basically designed for still fishing or moving very slowly. This would mean that persons who were buck-tailing flies behind a quickly moving boat would be "buck-tailing" and not mooching. It would mean that somebody who is trolling a plug-cut herring behind a boat at any speed would be mooching. It would mean that somebody who was trolling a live herring in the wake behind a boat would be mooching. A person using a downrigger would not be mooching. Strip-casting would have to be classified as a form of mooching because the gear has the appropriate terminal tackle for mooching and of course is capable of still fishing. Most people who strip-cast do it as a diversion from or as part of their mooching technique, in any event.

In the early part of the spring, late April and early May, the Coho are feeding on reddish euphausid shrimp in the water. It is almost impossible to catch them with a live herring, even a small one, because they are just not mature enough to take that type of bait. In those two months of the year mooching for Springs is frequently very difficult. Those who have been mooching unsuccessfully frequently remove their leaders and weights and put on a two-ounce sliding weight, a very small dodger, a foot and a half of leader, and a small red Tom Mack, since the Coho require a red lure because of the red feed. This combination is then trolled using the mooching rod and reel. But this, of course, is trolling and not mooching despite the fact that the tackle is mooching tackle but the answer here is that there is a dodger used and the set-up is not capable of being "mooched."

There is an understandable rivalry between moochers and trollers. The moochers take the position that theirs is the finer sport because there is usually just a very light weight and never any dodger, so the fish gives a fisherman a vastly superior fight and has a much greater chance of gaining its freedom. Surely the simple trolling of the mooching tackle should not be deemed to violate this code and therefore moochers need not be in the least offended simply because a fish is caught by trolling the tackle. Besides, one of the best of all systems of mooching as practiced from a car-top boat involves rowing hard for a short distance causing the baits to rise to the surface and then stopping and allowing the bait to swing or fall down in an arc which represents a falling or wounded herring and is very attractive to salmon. It is one of the cleverest of all mooching techniques, but certainly you could not accuse that person of trolling.

The term "mooching" should therefore include power mooching, strip-casting, plug-cut trolling at whatever speed and just plain old mooching. The terminal tackle must be capable of being used while still fishing whether it be a spoon, a herring strip or a live herring. The use of a "buzz-bomb" lure would fall into the mooching category because the boat is still and the lure is designed to imitate a falling wounded herring which is most definitely a mooching technique.

The definition manages to retain the aesthetic quality, that personal touch so important to the moocher because in each case save power mooching he is personally involved in catching the fish. It is his hand which strikes the fish and sets the hook, and he plays the fish without the encumbrance of a dodger or heavy weight. Even in power mooching, while he does not set the hook, he does play the fish with true mooching tackle and with Coho will be lucky to land two fish out of five.

Mooching is very much like stream or river fishing in which the angler's eye and quickness of hand and sureness of feel all blend together to catch the fish. The troller simply throws out the tackle, puts the boat in gear, and drags the equipment along. After the first couple of times out, he will not even stop the boat to play the fish unless it is a big one, simply reeling it in on his sixty-pound test line with his huge reel and scooping it aboard as the boat continues its relentless prowl. Frequently the fish, if a small one, is dragged along behind the boat without the fisherman even knowing that he has hooked it. If it is undersize he has no opportunity to release it for it will be dead or nearly dead. An undersized salmon stands an excellent chance of living after being released by a moocher.

2

Some General Principles

You will want to know something of the fish which you will be pursuing, its range, life-cycle, and so on, but for now let us look at some of its habits from the point of view of sports fishing.

Have you ever seen a salmon lying in a river facing downstream? Not very likely. When the salmon does go downstream, it lets the current carry it backward a ways, still facing upstream, or it makes a short, cross-river dash from lie to lie.

The reasons for this are obvious. Its food will be carried by the water flow toward it and it wants to be looking in the right direction; again the gills are designed to take in water through the mouth and out from under the gill covers - the fish does not like the reverse process. Finally, its body streamlining is such that it should face upstream.

The same is true of tide-water salmon. Why should a salmon lie with his tail facing into the current? Well, the answer is that he will not lie in that fashion. Nor will he swim with the tide when the tide flow is heavy and, generally speaking, he likes to swim against the tide, both for the purposes of feed and comfort. His whole life battle centers around swimming against the current, up river, especially, of course, in the final ascent of the river to spawn and to die.

To mooch in such a way as to present your bait to the salmon from behind the salmon is a mistake. The fish is expecting the tide to sweep the bait to him from the front or at the least he expects to catch up to it from its rear. This must be remembered because it plays an important part in mooching - a part not yet fully understood nor appreciated. Your grasp of this fundamental and your ability to make it work for you will make a difference to your fishing. It is an underlying principle and not to be forgotten.

Remember when you trolled? Going in one direction you would have a strike, returning the opposite way you would have no luck. The wise troller trolls across the current, at an angle to it. That way the salmon, gifted with two eyes which see ahead and to the side of him, becomes aware of the lure and makes his decision. He likes to see that bait sweeping down towards him, not only because he was used to it in the stream, but because it is the natural way for the salt water to present his feed to him.

Senseless too, for the angler to present a bait which is too low for his prey. Salmon do not have eyes that pick up feed directly beneath them. However, the salmon deals with this disadvantage in two ways: he may swim along the very bottom where the terrain permits it, that is if the bottom is sandy or mud or flat, smooth rock incapable of concealing an enemy such as a lingcod; and he will swim with head down and tail slightly higher to gain a better view of objects in front of him.

Rarely are salmon actually seen in the ocean, but on those rare, beautiful occasions when they are seen, the observant angler generally learns much. Salmon in the ocean handle themselves much as do salmon in the river. They not only face into the current, they also swim up the current, moving left and right, following the swing and sway of it, moving at an angle across it sometimes to secure a quieter lie: rising sometimes above it for a moment's rest or moving down through it into a depression again for a quieter lie, watching for food to be swept to them, alert for predators from above and from below. They lie behind bottom configurations which simulate river rocks, giving protection from the heavy current but enabling the salmon to take any passing morsel. When feeding, salmon love the food-producing heavy currents where herring are swept to them; when resting they like a quiet bay or lie behind a shoal or point or island where the current is less swift.

Sometimes, like river or lake fish, they scout just below the surface, mouthing little needle fish or inch-long herring. They will sometimes swim a foot below the surface rising to pick off individual herring. Like lake fish, they love water plants such as a kelp bed or eel grass where they can mosey along nibbling on all the little kelp and grass dwellers. They like to be where the feed is or where it will be brought to them; boiling, snapping tide currents, tide lines, channel points, islands, anywhere where the current is brisk but also affords the salmon a lie from which he can hunt.

When feeding he will sometimes sweep up or around his lie and range left and right looking for herring, moving against the current but sometimes traversing it from side to side until he finds his quarry. He will then feed and move ahead to a new lie, some quiet place where the current is not so swift, there to digest his meal but ever alert for food being swept to him by the current. A Chinook will seldom overindulge; a Coho will gorge until his sides bulge and herring are falling from his mouth. Both species are keen hunters. Both are attracted to a turning propellor, probably because experience has taught them that any violent turbulence in the water will produce dean or stunned feed. At Horseshoe Bay in Howe Sound you can see the moochers move in right alongside the docked ferries, allowing their baits to tumble. and roll in the ferry wake - often successfully.

The ocean bottom has as complicated a topography as a river bed, albeit on a larger scale. Learning to read that bottom is part of the moocher's art.

If your depth sounder shows a blurred depth reading, that is to say, the marking signal is wide or indicates several points of reflection, it means you are above a bumpy, rock-strewn bottom. Such an area is generally poor for mooching because the young salmon have learned that such areas mean danger and frequently death, either from sculpins or rockcod or lingcod and so as an adult he stays well above them or away from them altogether. You may therefore take it to be a basic principle that salt-water salmon do not like a rock bottom. If the shoreline or your depth sounder indicates the bottom is tumbled rock or rock-strewn, you are going to have to move a little further out or get to where it is smooth. Ideally, the salmon likes a sandy or mud bottom or at the very least a solid rock bottom that is incapable of concealing an enemy. Remember that the fish you are seeking has not always been as big or as fast as he is now. He has had to put in several years in the salt water surviving no end of predators. You need little imagination to realize that as a six-inch grilse he would not have lasted very long swimming near the natural habitat of a variety of cod, snappers and wolfeels. The number of salmon that we catch which have scars and deformities indicates beyond question that their lives are a constant battle with predators.

In addition, I have frequently tested this proposition by anchoring over a boulder-strewn bottom under ideal salmon fishing conditions. No matter how much effort was put in or the length of time spent I have yet to catch a salmon near the bottom in this type of terrain. By lifting the anchor and moving away from the boulder-strewn bottom, by as little as one hundred feet, my success factor has improved from nothing to reasonably good fishing almost immediately.

More will be said about herring and their habits in a later chapter, but you must know that in general salmon are likely to be in areas where there are herring. For their part herring like to take refuge where the tide flow is at a minimum. They are therefore found most frequently in bays or lying behind points where the current is eddying. They also take refuge on the lee end of shoals and reefs and in kelp beds and along the shore almost anywhere. Strangely enough, herring will frequently lie right out in the middle of an area that to the fisherman has no significance at all. The area doesn't seem to be behind a point and it doesn't seem to be in the lee of anything but the herring are nevertheless there and can be seen flipping on the surface. The reason for this is that the hearring are happy with the current flow in that particular spot, either because it suddenly becomes very much deeper or it is a confluence of currents that to the boater are inexplicable. These schools are found by watching for bird activity.

Another basic principle is that salmon like to rise to the bait and then fall back into the security of deeper water. You must therefore always fish the "drop-off." This principle applies wherever you are. Watch your sounder as you approach the area that you are going to fish or, if you do not have a sounder, start fishing and use your line as a gauge. Where the underwater terrain drops off is where you should fish. This principle is so acute that a difference of twenty feet can mean the difference between catching your limit and catching nothing. The salmon lie and travel just where the bar or ledge or shoal or rock cliff drops off. If you are fishing on the shoal or shallow part as opposed to being right on the edge or drop-off, you will have a poor time of it.

This is why sometimes you will find yourself alongside another boat that is really hitting the fish while you are catching nothing. The reason for this is that he has anchored so that his boat is weaving back and forth across the drop-off while you are fishing either too far from the drop-off in the sense of being over the deep water, or else you are fishing in water that is too shallow for the salmon. This particular factor is absolutely critical.

Another important principle, almost unknown, is that all salmon and especially Spring salmon need a point of reference. They are always where they are for some particular reason. If the foreshore drops off steeply, then you should fish right up against the wall because usually the salmon will be following that wall.

By "right up against the wall" I mean forty or fifty feet from the wall. If you are too close to the wall you will spend your time catching rockcod so you have to judge it nicely. Here too, the "ledge principle" applies. For some reason many steep rock walls have ledges eighty to one hundred feet down that run out from the walls then drop off abruptly to much greater depths at a point about one hundred feet from the rock wall itself. Fish these drop-offs.

When fishing close to a rock bluff with a steep drop-off always have a line up near the surface, somewhere between forty and sixty feet, because although the drop-off may be down at one hundred and twenty feet or so, the salmon are very conscious of the fact that feed is frequently much nearer the surface. Although they are traveling along that drop-off they don't mind rising a fair distance to nail a herring.

For their part, herring like the shorelines and are frequently right up against the shore. This is probably why the salmon keep close. Where you have an underwater shelf there are frequently herring above it; salmon traveling along the lip will rise to take them.

If there is a gently sloping beach running out from the shore, try to find where that drops off and fish there.

Frequently you will hear someone speak of a good Spring "hole" as though there were a deeper spot on the ocean floor into which Spring sink and lie. Most such "holes" are well named and in a bay, particularly, a hole is a good bet. Most fishable bays have depths of water going to two hundred feet. Since the salmon like security and like to see what is above them, they will frequently lie in a depression.

Bay fishing is different, too, for another reason. Herring may be anywhere. Their absence on the surface means nothing. There may be a long school lying against one shore or moving along a bluff or traveling down the center or lying in the center.

Here, despite the presence of other fishermen hovering over their favorite spots you must use your imagination. First determine the flow of the tide. If it is coming into the bay, the salmon are going to spend as little time as possible with their tail to the tide; they will usually enter the bay down the sides where the current is the reverse of the heavy flow entering the bay. If there is a group of boats on the left as you enter, then fish the edge of the pack nearest the mouth of the bay. They are probably packed together because someone has hooked a fish in that spot. In choosing the edge nearest to the mouth of the bay on an incoming tide you have a better chance of having the salmon see your bait first because he will be slipping in from the side where the water is actually running out of the bay.

If in doubt as to the current flow, watch your line as it goes down. Alternatively, fish the center of the bay right in the mouth because after entering the salmon will frequently make a swing to put himself facing into the incoming tide, hopefully sweeping herring in with it. Always fish the outside of the pack for this reason. If you have arrived first and chosen a spot next to the wall, then try to maintain a position which puts you first in line for whatever comes in. On an outgoing tide, reverse the process.

The question arises as to what to do if nobody is catching anything. The lazy fisherman is generally a hungry fisherman. You will find yourself torn between waiting out a spot you know that is good, hoping that a salmon will come in, or moving to a different spot. Generally speaking the answer is to put in that extra effort and move. Pull up your anchor and try some different spots. For this reason drift mooching is far superior to being anchored. To bring in that heavy anchor through one hundred and some odd feet of water is a lot of work and most people just sit it out and wait. On the other hand, if you are drifting it is an easy matter to try a different spot. Obviously you can not drift mooch if the wind or the tide are too strong because they will sweep you along so quickly your lines will be on the surface. Nevertheless, if at all possible avoid the use of an anchor. Drift mooching is doubly advantageous because your bait and your boat are sweeping toward the salmon as they should be.

No matter where you are, if you do spot a school of herring, fish the outside of the school. Never move your boat into it. More about this later, but for now, remember to fish from fifty to a hundred feet away from the school, on the outside of it wherever it is and remembering the tide. If you can feel the herring hitting your line, then move. Herring you can see on the surface run generally to about thirty feet in depth. Fish therefore from thirty to sixty feet down.

One facet of human behavior that is worth mentioning here, and which you will notice, is that if you are the first boat to arrive in an area and anchor you will find that all subsequent boats anchor at or near the same spot where you are. Even if you happen to have chosen the wrong spot. Your choice will be reinforced simply because others have followed your lead.

If, however, you are not catching anything and neither is anybody else, then pull up your anchor and move. The reverse of this process means that if you arrive to find a group of boats fishing in what you think is the wrong spot, ignore them and fish where you think it should be good. The boats that you are observing are probably fishing in that particular place simply because the first boat anchored there. You will be amazed at the effectiveness of a little original thinking on your own part. This applies particularly in open areas where it is difficult to find the local "hot spot."

The one boat that you can expect to be right on target is the charterboat. His years of experience, his expensive depth sounder, his knowledge of the tide and his ability to line up points of land will generally put him exactly where he wants to be. Give him lots of room, by all means, but anchor near him. Courtesy here requires that you keep a sensible distance from him. If the area is new to you then circle him at least once using your depth sounder to ascertain the terrain and to calculate why he is fishing where he is. After you have figured out the logic of his positioning, then take your boat and put yourself closer to the fish swimming aginst the current or, in the case of a bluff or a shoal, go further along the drop-off using the same principle.

There is an island in one area we fished with a long shoal running from one end. For years we fished with the other boats along the westerly drop-off of the shoal where it goes from forty feet suddenly to one hundred and twenty feet. One beautiful July morning we went out to fish this spot and found that there were so many boats there that it would make fishing difficult. There was almost no wind and a very slight tide running so we intended to drift mooch but the presence of so many boats was going to make that difficult.

We looked the situation over. There is nothing more difficult than to be original in your thinking process. To do the "different thing" is tough because there is always that sense of despair which tells you that your new idea has probably been tried a hundred times and has proven to be unsuccessful. The temptation is to adhere to the known successful method. I think what finally convinced us to fish elsewhere was that fishing had been good and we were not under any real pressure to catch anything for any reason and we resolved to fish a new spot just really to be away from the crowd. We arrived at the rather obvious deduction that if the shoal dropped off on the western side of the island there must be a drop-off coinciding with the eastern side of the island. We therefore turned tail and headed for the eastern drop-off. We didn't have a depth sounder and we had to keep trying for the bottom, searching for the shoal drop-off. It was much further out than we had anticipated and by the time we finally found where the drop-off was we were out of herring. Rockcod abounded on the shoal as did lingcod and the morning's fishing concluded with just a couple of ling lying in the fishtank.

Next morning we tried again, having the benefit of the previous day's efforts to our advantage. What a day! We limited in just under two hours. They were all Spring and as a bonus we had three really huge lingcod. We fished that drop-off for three long and happy years, when the weather permitted, before its advantages became known. There were two other boats that fished it during this period, both belonging to local fishermen who had made the same discovery that we had and were taking full advantage of it. The problem with a new spot is that people will see you playing fish from time to time and they will stop and give the spot a try. The next time you are out there that boat is there and a friend of his and perhaps one other and all of a sudden the new fishing hole is just as crowded as the one you gave up. That is, however, part of the sport and presents the challenge of finding yet another place that proves successful.

Interestingly enough, almost the same thing happened on the same shoal but in a different way. Two enterprising charter boatmen, Al Davidson of CKNW Fame and his charter boat captain, Al Christie, discovered that the western shoal ran out at one hundred and twenty feet after the first drop-off from forty feet for about half a mile and then abruptly dropped off again to a depth that was right off their sounder. They began to fish that drop-off, putting their limit aboard with great regularity and facility for they are good fishermen. Because their boat is well known, the new fishing spot became, almost overnight, a popular fishing hole. It continues to be a "hot spot" to this day.

Shoal fishing is interesting. The salmon lie along the drop-off but when the feed is thick they will gradually work their way up onto the shoal, cruising along the bottom in water that is only twenty or thirty feet deep and picking off the herring until gorged.

One day we saw a Coho which was so stuffed that in trying to swallow my herring which was within easy sight, he dropped three smaller ones which were still struggling in his mouth. He took my herring down as though it were the olive in the bottom of a martini and having made that mistake, we were able to find, when we had boated him, that his stomach held thirty-one small herring. He was so gorged on herring that they were forced from his maw by the weight of his own body as he lay on the bottom of our boat.

These salmon that are out sweeping the shoal are very difficult to catch because the water is so shallow. Generally you will have to resort to troll-mooching, which will be explained in a later chapter. The alternative to this is to drift mooch with your bait very near to the bottom. The problem with this latter technique is that you will be plagued by rockcod.

Salmon often travel in pairs and if you hook and play one you should pay particular attention to your other rod tips because the chances are you will catch the second one. Usually they are a buck and a doe and will be about the same size.

Another phenomenon that you should be aware of and should watch for is the mooch that will come while you are actually playing a fish. In order to fully understand why this phenomenon occurs, it is necessary to understand the basic feeding principles of both Spring and Coho. These will be contrasted in detail later, but for now it will suffice if you understand that when a Spring encounters a school of herring, he does not usually approach them only to pick off the odd herring. Instead he bulls his way through the school of herring thrashing left and right, stunning, maiming and killing by impact. He then circles and "mooches" under the school of herring picking up his casualties daintily. Other salmon, both Spring and Coho, take advantage of the enterprising Spring's work; they pick off the cripples, trying to reach them before he does, moving along behind him so that when he turns he often finds them reaping his harvest. Fellow Spring salmon must present much less of a problem for him than the aggresive Coho. A Coho eats quickly, almost frantically, devastating the individual herring and sometimes tearing it in half if two Coho are fighting over a single herring.

The dodger or flasher used by trollers, with its bait or lure trailing behind, triggers this feeding reflex in salmon because the dodger or flasher moves in such a way as to imitate a barging Spring while the bait behind the dodger simulates the crippled herring. Whoever invented the dodger knew his fish and his fishing. Most people do not understand the principle involved. The dodger is thought by many to imitate a school of herring flashing on the surface. In fact, the dodger imitates that large Spring producing cripples as he barges his way through the herring.

To return for the moment to the mooch that you can expect while playing a salmon, let's just apply the above reasoning to the situation. Your flashing salmon, the one you are playing, will often attract others because they take him to be "working" a school of herring. You should therefore leave your other baits in the water, most properly from twenty-five to forty feet deep and hope for the best.

There is much to be learned in the playing of a salmon and you should take a moment when you have one that you feel is well hooked to watch his actions in the water and perhaps even give him slack line for that purpose.

The general principles set out in this chapter will be refined and sometimes repeated later in this book but have been outlined here in general form so that later chapters will be more readily understood.

3

Let's Tackle Up

There are nearly as many varieties of rods, reels and lines as there are opinions as to which of these is best for the individual. People are different. People come in many shapes and sizes and are of different physical proportions. People, too, are of different temperaments, some being sensitive by nature regardless of their size or strength and others being more casual or indifferent, even insensitive. For this reason there is no one particular rod or reel that will be or can be declared "the best."

One day while waiting out a squall over a bowl of hot soup and crackers, watching the rain drip from the shingles along the roof-edge above the window, I fell to talking with an older man, a moocher, who was nursing a coffee along, obviously anxious to return to his fishing and watching the shingle edges even more intently than we others.

He explained that his doctor did not like him to mooch and had gone so far as to restrict him to three hours a day unless he had a sleep after the first session in which case he was allowed another three hours at the most, preferably two. He said that when he mooched he was in a constant state of excitement, even without a salmon on his line, and the difficulty was compounded because he smoked, which heightened his excitement and raised his blood pressure even more, frequently giving his chest pains, angina. He told us he had to give up liquor years before, after the first heart attack, but refused to stop either smoking or mooching. He said that he could not think of a better way to go than with a fishing rod in his hand.

At the other end of the spectrum there are people who will throw out the anchor, put their rods over the side and proceed to wine and dine and even sleep, leaving the fish to hook itself, which they occasionally do.

Obviously tackle preferences will vary with the individual. The opinions you will encounter will vary with the individual. Opinions, too, are colored by what people become used to using. If you learn how to mooch using a certain weight and length of rod, you will tend to stay with that type of tackle.

The locale where you mooch may affect your choice of tackle because if you need six ounces of weight to get down through the current to the bottom, you will most definitely want a somewhat heavier rod than you would use for an ounce and a half weight. If you are the type of person that really gets a bang out of using light tackle for Coho, then again a different rod is required and probably a different reel.

There is, however, a common denominator for mooching tackle - a norm which lies between light and heavy. It is this type of rod which is probably the one you should seek if you are just commencing to mooch.

Before throwing your dollars on the counter, you must find the right counter. Pick a neighborhood sporting goods shop at a time of day when it is not packed. Avoid lunch hours and Friday afternoons. Ask the man behind the counter if he is a moocher. (The fact that he has a gleam in his eye and his eye on the clock is not always a sure indication.)

If he gives you an emphatic "yes" and launches into a conversation with you, it may be assumed that it is safe to continue.

If he parries your question by asking you what you want to know, be leary. He may know what he is talking about or he may not. Listen to his opinions, get his prices, but unless he convinces you beyond any doubt that he knows what he is talking about, you should try somewhere else. You can always come back.

You should not buy your rod on the first day that you shop for it in any event. Just look, listen and learn. You can always return. If you have a choice at any time between two items that suit your purpose, you should always buy the more expensive one.

Given proper care your rod and reel will last half a lifetime or longer so it is senseless to buy cheap or doubtful tackle.

You will need a mooching rod. There are many brands, but the three top names at present are Hardy, Fenwick and Daiwa. The Hardy ten-foot moocher is a magnificent rod, sensitive in the tip but with enough spine to handle four or even six ounces of weight if needed. You should look at this rod as being one of the best on the market, but you will find that it is expensive. On the other side of the coin, the Daiwa gives you a ten-foot rod for considerably less money. It is an extremely popular rod and I am sure that it could be argued that it is not worth paying the extra money to get a Hardy. The difference between the two rods is, however, substantial.

Nearly all the modern mooching rods are made of fibreglass. There are some on the market made of the new graphite compositions but I have had no experience with these. Fibreglass rods are capable of great strength if used properly. Remember that they crush easily so care must be taken in this regard. Car doors are fatal, nor can you step on them or press them hard against any corner. They should be stored in a safe place.

Remember that a well-made rod has the glass running all the way through the cork handle to the butt-box. It does not have a wood or metal tube anywhere in the handle section. The cork handle should be affixed to glass all the way down to the butt end. The cork handle then should bend throughout its full length. Some rod makers and clerks will tell you that the rod needs a metal tube handle for strength or spine, but don't you believe it. By the time the glass is down to the cork handle it has all the spine that it needs. Nor should you heed the clerk who tells you that a wood or metal plug is needed in order to mount the reel-seat. This is just not so. A wooden plug or metal tube is neither needed nor desirable. It is often the sign of a cheap rod.

Very few rods have movable reel seats which is unfortunate because the movable seat has several distinct advantages over the fixed type. Being able to adjust the reel forward or backward, even a few inches, can make all the difference in your reeling speed and comfort. Also it is sometimes necessary to be able to offset your reel to one side so that your line winds into your reel evenly if you are a person who tends to reel with the reel canted.

There is a drawback to the movable seat and that is that frequently mounting your reel in the movable seat will damage the cork handle. It is sometimes necessary to apply tape under the place where you are going to fix the reel or even a curved metal shim. When buying a rod with a movable reel seat you have to be sure that that particular reel seat will take the reel that you are going to buy and you should check that right in the store.

Your mooching rod can double as a steelhead rod of the very first order providing it has a movable reel seat. That most beautiful of steelhead reels, the Silex, is mounted near the butt, but the now famous Ambassadeur series is mounted further forward while the coffee grinder or French spinning reel is mounted somewhat in between these two extremes. The Silex and Amassadeur both use the same first guide as does a mooching rod, but the coffee grinder requires a large spinning guide. This is easily installed.

Fenwick rods are excellent rods and have the singular advantage of being available in blanks. That is to say, you can buy the glass tube and make your own rod. Do not discard this suggestion as being beyond your capabilities. It is easier to make up your own rod than it is to set up a Christmas tree. It takes a little more time, but it really does not take very much more skill. You can obtain a Fenwick 1262 blank for very few dollars and the hardware, depending upon the quality, will cost you just a little more. It is fun to do, not too messy and not at all difficult.

The rod that you are seeking must be stiff enough to enable you to set a hook and yet sensitive enough in the tip to signal the presence of a salmon at your bait.

Some speak of a rod as being a "fast" rod. By this is meant that it returns from a flexed position to the straight, normal position quickly. This is an important quality when you are handling a leaping Coho because you want the line to stay tight to him at all times. A weak, slow rod often allows the fish to throw the hooks because he has slack line.

Your mooching rod should be light in weight and flexible throughout its entire length. The typical trolling rod is short and stiff with no flexibility to speak of. The tip is all spine. A fly-rod has an extremely sensitive tip but it has no spine or stiffness to hold the two-ounce weight and does not have enough stiffness to enable you to set you hook. If there is one single fault to which most mooching rods fall heir, it is in the fact that the tip does not have enough spine. A delicate balance must be struck here because if the tip is too stiff, that is to say, if it has too much spine, it will often not be sensitive enough to signal the mooch. The tip that you want must be able to support a two or three-ounce weight without drooping over like a wet piece of spaghetti. It must be still enough to hold that weight and still have enough in reserve to signal the slightest touch on your herring. Chuck Jones, a moocher of some considerable talent, boasts that his Fenwick rods will tell him whether his herring is inhaling or exhaling. That's the sort of sensitivity that you are looking for.

Here is something that you can do; take the Hardy ten-foot moocher in one hand, another rod of your choice in the other and tremble your hands just enough to make the rod tips move about half an inch remembering the Hardy is supposed to be the Cadillac. Watch the tips and feel the rods tremble concentrating on spine, sensitivity and that ability to bend for its entire length, remembering that it must be light in weight. You may not want to buy the Hardy but it will give you an indication of what your rod of choice should be able to do. Some people find the ten-foot ten-inch Hardy is much too heavy a rod and if it has a fault, it lies in this area. On the other hand, it will handle up to six ounces of weight and still have enough sensitivity to let you know what is happening, even to the extent of the slightest touch.

If you are lucky enough to be able to borrow a friend's rod for the weekend, then by all means do so. Check the make and the length and see how it performs. There are many different makes and I have not tried them all. Your choice of rod is very important so take your time.

Your reel must be a single action reel, which means that it takes one turn of line in for each single turn of the reel handle, there being no gears involved. In the old days the best reel around was the Windex. Then they stopped making them and the market was flooded with cheap imitations. Today, fortunately, there are a number of excellent reels on the market without getting into the Windex imitations. Daiwa has some good reels; the Hardy "Longstone" is a beauty, but expensive. There are others, American, Australian and Japanese which are also quite good. Buying a reel is tricky; there are so many things to look for, it is difficult to tell you where to start. You must look at the reel very carefully, noting the workmanship and the balance of the spool. Does the lever that engages and releases the ratchet work smoothly? Are there any projections that would enable the line to catch? Don't forget to ask the shop where you are buying the reel if they repair that reel and whether or not they have spare parts. Once again I am driven to say that the Hardy reel is probably the Cadillac of the available reels and should be used for comparison purposes. Remember that there must be a very close tolerance between the turning spool and the case so that the line will not slip in between. The handles must be sturdy and the workmanship careful.

The choice of a reliable line is made difficult by reason of the fact that there are almost as many opinions as to which is the best line as there are lines. The biggest seller by far is "Charterboat" which is a supple greenish-colored nylon sold in many different tests (strengths) at a very reasonable price. This nylon is packaged in a coil with just a touch of aniseed oil. Anise has an odor which has been proven to be neutral to fish and may even attract them. From time to time you can buy small bottles of a compound containing anise-seed oil to put on your hands before you handle your tackle. It is not often available in the stores.

Commercial fishermen use it and swear by it. My tackle box is coated with the ointment type and I still have a jar of it around to touch on my hands before I tackle up. In any event, the line is covered with it and this keeps it supple and it also removes any odor problem from the nylon and the feeling among most fishermen is that some nylons are not liked by the salmon. Bell nylon is excellent.

In theory your main line should be about five pounds heavier in test than your leaders so that when you catch on the bottom or elsewhere the leader will break before the main line does. There is a substantial degree of convenience in using the same main line as your leaders and when you are doing a great deal of fishing, this is generally the practice. It enables you to tie your leaders from the same test line as your main line and this can be quite handy. You will lose the odd weight when the line snaps above the weight, but that happens very seldom.

The argument then develops as to what test you should use for your leader. Most moochers agree that fifteen or twenty-pound test is a sensible weight for your main line, but there is a school of though that argues for extremely light leaders. These moochers insist that the lighter the leader, the more chance of having a mooch. They agree that it is more difficult to land the fish because of the lighter leader but argue that here skill enters to make the contest interesting. The same argument is made by steelheaders who say the light leader is needed in low, clear water.

While color of leader may be important in low water or indeed in any stream, the weight of the leader is in my opinion of little importance. The steelheaders working the Atnarko and Skeena for the really big Chinook use fifty-pound test line and leader but count the leader calibre as being of no concern whatsoever and, within limits, I have had the same experience with Coho and Spring in the ocean.

As for mooching - my tests indicate that you can use leaders of up to fifteen-pound and perhaps twenty-pound test without affecting the quality of your mooching.

You will find if you use leaders of nylon in excess of twenty-pound strength that you must use a very high quality line such as Trilene salt water monofilament because cheaper lines in excess of twenty-pound test are so thick that they impair the natural movement of the herring.

Over twenty years of intensive fishing summer and winter I have tested ordinary fifteen-pound Charterboat nylon against every conceivable light leader material available in six pound test, which is the lowest that it seems to me you can go and still have a fair chance of landing the fish.

These tests indicate that there is no increase or decrease in the frequency of mooches when you use the lighter nylon. On any given day you may find one rod taking all of the fish, but mooch for mooch, day after day, the tests indicate that the mooches balance out. There were days when all of the fish were caught on the rod having the fifteen pound test and there were no mooches at all on the six pound test leaders. This difference in the takes on two different rods is a matter which will be mentioned later, but the tests seem to indicate that leader strength has little to do with it. Such exhaustive tests cannot be based upon a few days fishing or a week's fishing; to be a fair test it has to be carried out for at least a year under all conditions and you must consciously keep track of the lighter leader success by writing down the actual number of definite mooches for each leader. From time to time you will hear of some fellow really knocking them dead using light line. The fact is that he would probably do just as well with fifteen-pound test leader.

On the other side of the coin the disadvantages of using light leader are legion. The first disadvantage is that it nicks easily. You can nick it while tying the leader or while it sits in your tackle box or on the side of a boat or in a thousand different ways. Put even a slight nick or rub in six-pound test leader and it will break at the slightest strain. Exactly the same nick in fifteen pound test line will not impair it to any degree because it is so very much thicker. This is another reason for staying away from expensive very fine line. Fifteen-pound test Charterboat or comparable is no stronger than other fifteen pound test line that is finer, but it takes a great deal more rough use and can stand nicks and scratches better.

Nowhere is this more evident that when you catch your first lingcod. A lingcod is a beautiful fish, highly sought after and fun to catch. These fish have a great set of teeth, however, and will nick your line nearly every time. After you have boated it you have to check your leader for nicks, of course, before baiting up again. Nine times out of ten it will be badly nicked and indeed we never, ever leave a leader on when we have brought in a ling unless just one hook has been caught at the very outside of the mouth. If you hook that same ling on six pound test or on very fine fifteen pound test, you will lose him five times out of six.

Then, too, there is the dogfish problem. These beautifully horrible members of the shark family have razor-sharp teeth that sever fine nylon almost at the first touch. It is very annoying to bring up your tackle after a gentle tug, or whatever, to find your hooks are gone. You will always have that nagging doubt as to whether or not it was a dogfish and this can truly by annoying, but also the dogfish tend to stay around and really should be brought to the surface and killed for that reason alone. They are in no danger as a species, just the reverse in fact, and can seriously interfere with your mooching. Killing them is accomplished by stabbing them or cutting them open. Contrary to some opinions, this does not attract other dogfish. There will be more on dogfish later, but for now, beware of using too light a leader.

Finally, light nylon suffers from the very real disability of losing you a good many salmon. Both Coho and Chinook have sharp teeth which can easily fray lines. Using light nylon means that you have to be very careful in playing your fish — the line can and will wear at the knot and sometimes becomes pinched in the treble hooks when the fish swims into the leader.

A salmon with one or two hooks left in his mouth is not a dead salmon by any means, but it is probably very uncomfortable for him.

One afternoon we took five big Chinooks, all over fifteen pounds, off the tip of the Ballenas Islands and found that three of the five had hooks in their mouths. Two sets of these were mooching tackle and the other a single hook from a large Tom Mack spoon - probably a commercial troller. Each time we find someone else's tackle in a salmon we try, naturally, to find out why the tackle broke. There is nearly always light test nylon left on the hooks and by light nylon I mean ten pound test and down. The second most frequent cause seems to be improperly tied knots. The fact that three of the five of these salmon had tackle in them was an unusual occurrence, but it is not at all an unusual occurrence to bring in a salmon with a mooching hook embedded in the jaw. Examination of these hooks and the nylon attached indicates, almost without exception, that the line has broken due to being nicked on the teeth or because the knot was poorly tied.

To summarize, then, buy a main line consisting of about four hundred and fifty or five hundred yards of fifteen or twenty-pound test line. Buy another spool for leaders either of the same test or just a little but lighter. You could use twenty pound test main line and fifteen pound test for your leaders or exactly the same for each, in which case I suggest you use the fifteen pound test. Fifteen pound test leader will land almost anything you can hook, including forty, fifty and sixty pound lingcod.

Do not buy giant economy-size rolls of nylon monofilament. They are frequently unreliable and can cause trouble when you are tying your knots. Also, nylon is suspected of losing its strength with age, so the advantage of keeping a large roll in the basement is dubious.

Change your main line every year. From time to time we cut off the last thirty or forty feet of line when it starts to lose its tone and color during the fishing year.

Always retie your weight if you have subjected it to a long strain with a big fish or if you have caught bottom. Be sure to keep your rod somewhere safe where the line won't be stepped on or caught up on something or rubbed.

Hooks are a problem. The finest on the market were Mustad triple extra strong number 3567's, but something has gone wrong with their welding process and the weld is now very rough such that the third hook has a shoulder on it that cuts the line just as quickly as a knife. Perhaps this problem will be overcome, but watch those welds.

The next best hook is the Eagle-Claw. They are strong and well made and they are sharper than the Mustads. They are not quite as strong as the Mustads.

Some moochers use "Open Road" hooks, but these are considerably weaker than either Mustad or Eagle-Claw. They will do if there is nothing else, but generally speaking they are to be avoided. They will do for most fish but just when you want to land that really big one, you will find that sometimes the single hook that is holding the fish will straighten enough to enable the salmon to break loose.

Number six Mustad hooks always need to be sharpened so for years I have used a small whetstone to sharpen every point on every hook. Eagle-Claw do not have this disadvantage and are reasonably sharp.

To test the triple hook for strength, simply take two of the three hooks between your fingers and try to bend them together as though you were closing a clam shell. If they close easily, beware. Try the same thing with Mustad hooks, making sure that they are Mustad hooks right out of a box marked that way and you will have a good comparison.

For years the controversy has raged over what size of hooks to use and probably the real answer lies in using a variety, depending upon the type of fishing you are doing and the way the Spring are taking the bait. Moochers are in general agreement that two triple hooks tied about three inches apart seem to be the best hook-up, but it is the size of those hooks that is in doubt.

Hooks become smaller as the size of the number increases. Going the other way a number one is a big hook but then it goes one ought, two ought and each time the number increases, the size of the hook increases.

The controversy centers around the use of hooks sized six, eight and ten. Most moochers use number sixes, some few more use number eights, while a fairly large group uses tens. A six is almost twice the size of a ten. There is little doubt that the greater popularity of the size six triple hook is founded not in popularity or familiarity, but in its superiority. The moocher who uses tens stands a little better chance on a certain type of mooch, but all things considered, fish for fish, day after day, Coho or Chinook, the six is the wiser choice. You will find most charterboats using them as well as most moochers. Some moochers have turned to a single number ten triple hook in the nose of their herring for Coho fishing. This practice originated with and is carried on by certain charterboats. For the skipper of a charterboat to tie a single triple hook onto a leader takes about ten seconds; the tying of a good two-hook mooching leader takes about three minutes. The Coho's feeding habit is to tug at the tethered herring from the tail end, finally swallowing it tail first. There are exceptions to this, of course, especially when there are numerous Coho about in which case almost anything goes. The charterboats have found that in the hands of a novice who cannot read his rod tip, the single triple hook in the nose becomes quite effective because the Coho generally swallows the whole herring before the novice can react to his rod tip. All he has to do is play the fish because it has hooked itself. The ardent moocher, however, wants the couple hook setup because as he watches his rod tip, he has a chance at quite a number of fish using that second hook because he can see the "take" and react to it.

As to whether to use silver or bronze hooks - it seems to matter very little. My preference is a bronze because it blends in somewhat better than silver on the top side of the fish which is dark. Fish at close distances have incredibly sharp eyes. They will strike at all sorts of lures out of instinct such as a spoon that is tarnished or with the paint chipped because it is moving and it triggers their feeding instinct but the fact remains that a fish does have extremely good eyesight. We have had them occasionally strike at the bare hooks as we have pulled them in with the herring gone.

Imagine for a moment the eyesight and coordination needed for a twenty-pound fish to maneuver itself to strike at darting trolled lures moving along at five or six knots. The presence of visible hooks in a herring must therefore discourage some salmon and in my mind's eye bronze hooks would be less visible to the fish.

Mooching weights should be purchased in a number of sizes and you should have a few of the one ounce weights, a whole bunch of the ounce and a half, and quite a few two ouncers, a couple of threes and perhaps two four-ounce weights and one or two six-ounce weights. Of course, all this tackle will look so disorganized lying on the counter that you will probably treat yourself to a small tackle box to hold the weights, hooks, leader material, etc.

Having placed your purchases in the tackle box, do not forget that you will need a hook remover. This is a device that looks like a pair of pliers with a long nose, having a small beak at the end to grasp the hooks. They cost only two dollars or so and are invaluable. You will also need a knife and there is only one on the market that is worth bothering with. It is made by Frosst and costs about twelve dollars. It has a long stainless steel blade, a hard plastic handle rippled for good grip and a spoon at the handle end to remove the salmon's kidney which lies along the top of his stomach cavity.

Avoid all of the so-called boning knives, the fancy gerber blades, hunting knives and jack-knives of any kind. Your knife is important and you should not experiment. The Frosst is probably the only knife on the market that will really do the job. The gerber fish knives are a magnificent knife, but the steel is so highly tempered that it will frequently shatter as you are fileting the fish. You simply must have a long blade on your knife and it must be stainless steel and it must be tough, not brittle, and finally it must have a spoon on the end to be practical. The only knife that fits these requirements is the Frosst.

Very handy also is a pair of stainless steel fisherman's pliers to remove hooks from strange tough substances such as boat seats, the anchor rope and your hands.

If you really get into mooching you will want a horse's curry-comb to use as a fish scaler. It consists of a series of hoops attached to a red handle. There are four hoops, the biggest about the size of a coffee can. It costs only three dollars, but they are hard to find. They sure do scale a fish!

Just before you leave the tackle shop, buy a tube of reel grease, not oil.

At home take the reel apart before putting the line on. This is accomplished generally by undoing one small screw in the center of the reel on the spool side. Carefully take the screw out and just as carefully remove the nut or handle or whatever and then remove the washers placing them separately with the right side up as you take them off in a row in the exact order in which they came off. After you have removed each of these washers and placed them on the table facing up exactly the same way that they have been taken off the spindle, then remove the spool. Carefully grease the spindle and the ratchet gear and the ratchet mechanism and spring and generally everything that will be concealed when you put the spool back on. Put a little grease into the spool spindle hole, at the end that goes on to the spindle first. Then grease the washers on both sides, placing them back on the table the same way up that you lifted them. Grease anything else that takes your fancy but do not grease any exterior part of any section of the reel that will be exposed or that you will touch or that the line will touch and do not grease or oil the handles, of course. Now go wash your hands thoroughly so that they are free of all grease.

Reassemble the reel carefully making sure that you are holding it with a grease-free hand and using the other hand to carefully reassemble the reel, putting the washers back in the same order and the same side up as you removed them.

Go wash your hands again. Now wipe the reel removing all traces of any grease that could possibly have adhered to any surface anywhere. You will probably have made a mistake by putting a little too much grease in one area or another and you are going to have to wipe it off and you will get some grease on the reel, but be patient and remove the excess grease and you can even use a little soap on your cloth to remove all possible grease anywhere on the reel. Now you are ready to put your line on after once again washing your hands. Always tie the line to the spool. Sooner or later you will end up hauling your rod and reel up from the bottom and if your line has not been tied to the reel, it can sure be embarrassing. Wind the line onto the spindle of the reel in a cross-hatch pattern weaving it slowly back and forth across the drum; do not put it on too tightly, just firmly. The weaving is to prevent the taught line from cutting down into the line on the drum when you are playing a fish.

Again being careful, you can put a little vaseline on the reel mount where it will press against the reel seat on the rod and a touch on the nut and mechanism that will hold the reel on. Again wipe every trace of vaseline from your rod and reel and mounts. You should put vaseline or grease on your ferrule before assembling the rod especially if your rod has glass ferrules. In fact, probably the best substance to use on glass ferrules is candle wax. Failure to wax or grease glass ferrules will mean you will soon be the owner of a one-piece rod. Once bonded together nothing short of dynamite will separate them. If you are about to assemble your rod on a dock and do not have grease handy, simply rub the male end of the ferrule against the side of your nose and it will pick up sufficient body oil to ensure that it will come apart at some later time.

If your rod does not want to come apart, there is a method that is generally accepted as being better than most to separate the two parts. Simply pick the rod up and grasp each part as though you were going to take the rod apart by yourself, having one hand on each section. Now have your buddy do exactly the same thing while facing you as though he were also going to do it alone. Now both of you try to separate the rod and you will find that this is more effective than most assistance.

4

The Moocher's Knot
And How To Tie It

You can buy mooching leaders at almost any tackle store but they are expensive and frequently tied with a type of hook that is not satisfactory. Often the distance between the two hooks on the leader is not right for the size of herring you are using. Some of the mooching leaders you can buy have a sliding hook so that you can place it wherever you want to, but this type of hook-up is definitely unsatisfactory because when you come to set the hook, it will frequently give way.

To tie the leaders, you use the moocher's knot. This knot is tied in a variety of ways, but only one is correct.

You must have a good deal of patience in reading these instructions. Do not be downhearted if it seems difficult to grasp at first. A thorough understanding of the knot is necessary because you will be encountering people who will want to show you a different — easier, faster, better — way to tie it and unless you understand what the knot is and how it works, you will probably fall heir to a system of tying the knot that does not tie it properly.

The tying of these leaders is a pleasant task on a winter's evening. You will want to have a good supply of leaders in your tackle box and I generally keep about fifty or sixty leaders wrapped around toilet paper rolls because I find that convenient. Some fellows use cork boards which are sold in fishing goods stores and others wrap them around a single rolled-up piece of kleenex. Frequently when the fishing is good you will find the Springs are interspaced with dogfish and you will go through a substantial number of leaders. This was the case one day when we took sixteen Springs. We were mooching in one hundred and twenty feet of water and the fish were taking at forty-five and sixty feet, but for every one we hooked we had to play in at least two dogfish. We always cut the leader free and throw it away when we have landed a Spring because there is a high probability that the line will have been nicked and in any event it will, of course, have been subjected to a good deal of strain while playing the fish. It is just not worth it to lose the next fish for the cost and trouble of a leader.

   The mooching knot is listed in most knot books as "the salmon hook knot," and is really the basic knot for most salmon fishing. The problem is that although most knot books show you the way the knot is tied, they do not show you how to tie it and probably for a good reason. The tying of the knot is quite difficult by any standard. Once you have learned it, you can use it for nearly every type of hook-up used for river fishing or for salt water. The knot is used by steelheaders for most of their hook-ups and enables them to attach roe. It is used to tie the hook-ups for plug-cut trolling and for herring strip and for whole herring and for live herring. It is probably the strongest known way of attaching a hook to a nylon leader.

   The knot was shown to me by Peter Broomhall, who is an ardent and skilful steelhead fisherman. His kindness has enabled me to show dozens of others. You could ask your sporting store clerk to help you, but you are going to have to understand the knot to know whether or not he is showing you a correct variation. It always surprises me how few people know how to tie it although a good bet is a steelhead fisherman. They are almost a vanishing species!

   The knot consists of seven or eight turns of whipping which go over the line as it runs along the shank of the hook. The eye of the hook serves only to stop the whipping from slipping off the hook, but even that function may not be necessary if the whipping is tight enough. The knot is started by pulling about three or four feet of line from your monofilament spool. Slide one triple hook onto the line, being careful to put the line through the eye from the bottom of the hook. All triple hooks consist of one piece of wire bent into two hooks with the third hook being welded onto the first two. Your line must enter the eye from the same side as the third, welded on, hook (see illustration number one).

   Forget about this first hook, leaving it to sit threaded on the nylon. Now take a second triple hook and thread it onto the line in the same way, drawing about twelve or fourteen inches of line through the eye. Grasp the hook with your right hand if you are right handed, holding it by the eye in an upright position, that is to say, with the welded-on hook pointing downwards. Now take the fourteen inches of line and make a three-inch circle ending

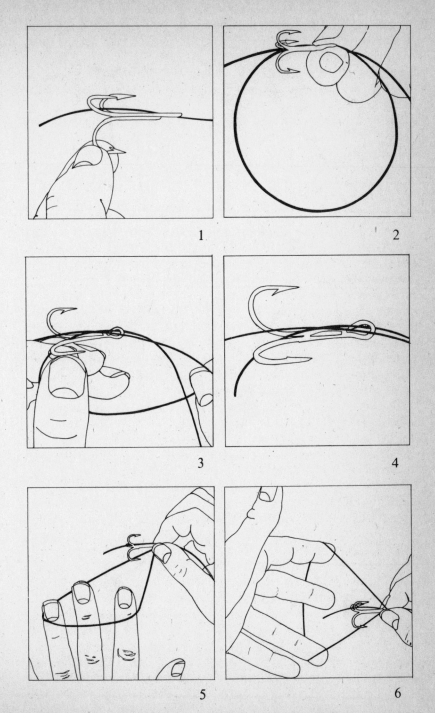

1

2

3

4

5

6

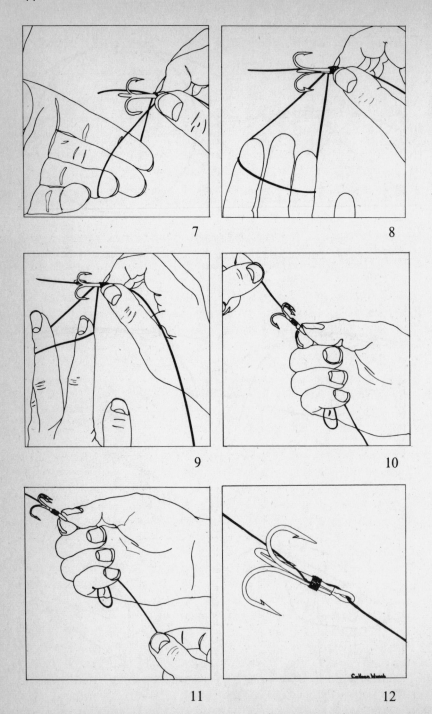

7

8

9

10

11

12

with the tail of the line lying between the two upright hooks of the triple hook pointing away from your right hand (see illustration number two).

The circle of line must not get over onto the other side of the eye. The line and circle must be on the side nearest to you or on the top of the hook, but that circle of line must never get over onto the other side of the eye (see illustrations number three and four).

Now grasp the eye and lines pinching them with thumb and forefinger to hold them in position and you are going to have to hold them really firmly.

Now take your left hand with your fingernails pointing towards you and put your three center fingers into the loop with your thumb and little finger doing nothing as in illustration number five.

What you must now do is to whip the line around the hook, always keeping the right-hand side of the loop rolling over the hook shank. The left-hand side of the loop will simply lie along the shank of the hook as you make the loops.

The whipping is done by rolling your fingers around the inside of the circle so that each time you throw the right-hand side of the circle around the shank you are whipping on a layer of line. The problem is that you have to know and to keep in mind which is the side of the circle that is doing the whipping and which is the side of the circle that is simply lying along the shank as the other line goes over it (see illustrations number six, seven, eight, and nine).

Always keep your fingers spread to hold the circle taut while rolling the line over the shank. Your fingers must always end up in the same position each time so that the right-hand side of the circle is the side that is doing the whipping. It takes a little practice and at first you will find that you do not have a good enough grip on the eye and the line and you will probably have to start the knot over.

If you do have to start the knot over, cut off your fourteen inches of line and start with nice crisp fresh nylon because there is nothing worse than trying to work with nylon that has been bent into some position that you do not want.

The number of loops varies but is never fewer than six and it is generally felt that seven or eight is about right, but you can put on as many as ten or twelve or fifteen if you wish. At this point the hook and line will look as it appears in illustration number nine. The loop goes over the tail each time, naturally.

After you have wrapped the hook then tuck the loop into your right hand and hold the loop out of the way with the bottom two or three fingers of your right hand against your palm, still holding the line and hook with your thumb and forefinger. All you are doing is getting the loop out of the way and keeping tension on it so that the wraps lie on the hook properly.

Now grasp the tail that has up until now simply been in your way and pull it. You will feel a little loop of line held by your thumb and forefinger slip through and pull tight. Then, still holding everything tight with thumb and forefinger of your right hand, let go of the tail and pull the main line gently, drawing the loop up inside the palm of your hand to disappear into the knot. It will want to catch on the hooks or your little finger, but just let it slide through until it pulls tight (see illustrations ten and eleven).

At this point in time you will be thinking that there is no possible way you will ever learn how to tie this knot. You will probably be imagining yourself spending your winter evenings learning the knot rather than tying it. A little persistence will pull you through.

After you have pulled the main line the knot should be in place and if it is not quite smooth you can use your thumbnail to flip the loops into place. Then grasp the tail and the main line and pull them to tighten the whipping on the shank. At this point you cut the tail off, but before you do so, pull it back between the barbs. This makes the knot stronger and also keeps your main line from being pinched in between the hooks when you are playing a fish. Illustration number twelve shows the knot completed but before the tail of line has been pulled between the barbs and cut.

Illustration number thirteen shows the actual knot as it might appear before tightening.

That completes the knot and you are now ready to proceed with the tying of the hook that you have slid on to the line. This is accomplished by repeating the entire operation and just completely forgetting about the hook that you have already tied on the end of the line. Just treat it as though it was not there. You just throw your loop over both sets of hooks and repeat the whole operation.

The distance between the two hooks has to be estimated and you will have to make it a little shorter than you actually want because when you have finished tying the knot by pulling the tail, you will be pulling out about half an inch of line being held by your thumb so the distance between the two hooks is increased by about that distance at the time that you pull that tail hook into place.

If you refer to illustration number thirteen, you will see the

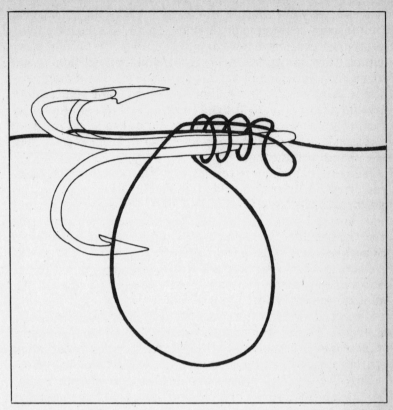

13

little curve of line that is held by the thumb and which is pulled out when you pull the tail and which adds to the distance between the two hooks. It is sometimes annoying when you are throwing your loop over to tie the second hook on to find that the loop tangles in the second hook which is dangling there. This problem can be avoided by snuggling the first hook up quite close to the second hook which you are tying and instead of leaving that little bend of line under your fingers, make that little loop ride around the ball of your right thumb which is holding the hook. You are simply giving yourself a little extra line to pull when you pull the tail. You then tie the knot and when you pull the tail the loop of line that you have ridden up over the ball of your thumb will slide off the thumb and give you the distance between the two hooks. A little experience will enable you to place the distance exactly.

If you are having difficulty with that left hand rolling the loop over, then you can stop at illustration number three which is the point where you have made the three-inch loop but before you have inserted your three fingers into the loop with your nails facing you. Instead of using your three fingers to fold the loop over, simply grasp the right-hand side of the loop which is the part of the loop that disappears into your right thumb and forefingers and wind it around the shank starting near the eye and winding away from it. You will have to bullfinch a little by using your bottom three fingers of your right hand to help you but you can do it. You can wrap the shank in this manner and then when you have it wrapped, again tuck the loop into your right-hand palm, pull the tail and then the main line.

The knot that you have just learned is the key to nearly every type of leader that you could ever possibly have to tie. It has endless uses. There are other ways to tie this knot but most of them are incorrect. When the knot is tied incorrectly the breaking strength decreases sharply. When it is tied properly it is the nearest thing to the full strength of the leader.

You may wish to vary the distance between your hooks to suit your herring depending on the time of year and what bait is available, but this will come quite easily to you as you progress in your facility with the knot. The same knot of course is used to tie on single hooks by themselves or in tandem for plug-cut fishing.

There is no other knot which will match this knot to tie a hook into the center of a line; if you want to try the sliding hook set-up, it is tied by using this knot and a completely separate piece of line for the loop. Instead of tying the knot into the leader you simply place the hook on the leader with or without running the line through the eye and use the spearate piece of line to whip the hook into place, pulling it tight of course, and you will find then that it slides on the line.

There is only one other knot that you need and that is the knot for securing your line to the swivel on your weight. The knot to use is the improved cinch knot which is quick and easy to tie.

Simply pass the line through the eye of the swivel and turn it back upon itself as in figure number one. Now twist that line around the main line six or seven times as in figure number two.

Now pass the end through the opening in the line which you have created by twisting the line as in figure number three.

Now pass the end through the second opening you have created, again as in figure three. Just before you pull it tight, it is wise to moisten it with your tongue because it makes the nylon slide easily.

This is a well-known knot which has been thoroughly tested and is generally reliable. It does have two dangerous aspects; the line must be wet before you pull it tight and secondly, it is fatal

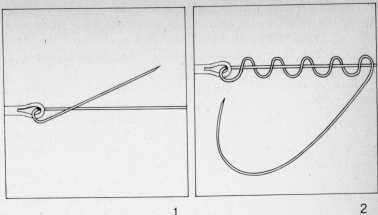

1

2

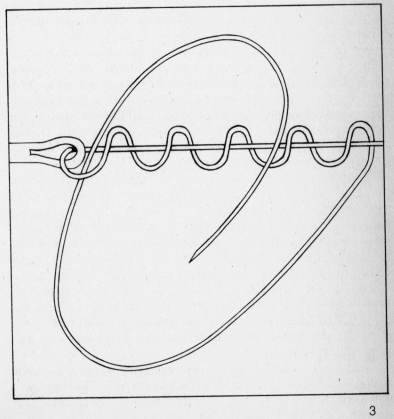

3

not to pull it really tight before you rely on it. If your line is bleached or defective, the knot will snap as though the nylon were rotten and that is the reason for pulling it good and tight. If it does not break, then you know you have got it right and that your line is in good shape.

If your line snaps when you pull the knot tight, examine the line carefully. Sometimes the knot is cranky and it snaps for no particular reason but generally the line is rotten and you should then pull off thirty feet or so and put that in your garbage can. Then re-tie the knot.

Never throw lengths of nylon overboard. From an ecology point of view it is not nice to have the bottom littered with all sorts of lengths of nylon — it bothers scuba divers — but there is another reason and that is that frequently the piece of line you throw overboard ends up wrapped around your propellor which will, if it gets into the seals, ruin your outboard leg just as surely as if you took an axe to it.

Where the propellor shaft goes into the housing of the leg, there are a variety of different types of bearings. If you allow a piece of nylon to wrap itself around the shaft it will frequently work its way under the bearing surfaces and allow water up into the leg and in no time at all you will burn out the bearings. Some marinas actually have legs which have succumbed to this type of problem mounted on the wall so that you can see how absolutely dangerous nylon is on your propellor shaft.

Frequently you will find that your line does catch on the propellor. It is always a good idea if you are anchored to leave your propellor in gear because the current, when the boat is being held stationary, turns the propellor which will sometimes catch your lines. If you do catch your line in the propellor and cannot get it off, then lift your leg out of the water as far as you can and cut the line off above the leg. Then take your gaff and fish for the end of the line that has the weight and bait on it and pull that up until you have hold of it. Now gently pull that piece allowing the propellor to turn and allowing the line to be pulled free of the shaft. It has to be out of gear to do this but it is really the only way to get all of the nylon off the shaft.

Incidentally, tests show that the best way to tie a knot for strength is to pull it tight at the time that you tie it. Do not leave any knot loose or less than absolutely tight on the premise that the fish will tighten it for you.

The first knot explained in this chapter is a difficult knot to tie and I sincerely hope that you stay with it until you have it. The knot has always fascinated me. I recall one day when a friend came to the cabin where we were staying for our summer mooching holiday and explained that he and three other fellows were on their way to Rivers Inlet; they wanted to learn the knot for their plug-cut leaders. I went aboard his boat and with his friends clustered about, demonstrated the knot. One fellow caught on the first time it was shown and a second fellow had it in hand on his third or fourth try and the third caught on after a fifth or sixth attempt. One fellow simply went into the galley and poured himself a drink.

An interesting thing happened arising out of this particular incident. The fellows aboard went off up to Rivers Inlet but stopped over at Stuart Island to fish for a day or two. The dock was buzzing with stories of giant Spring which were snapping twenty-pound leaders with great regularity, and a Stuart Island guide was working on a steel leader. He was determined not to lose another one of these big Springs. One fellow to whom I had shown the knot remembered that it is absolutely imperative that it be tied exactly right or the bigger fish will pop the leader just as things are really happening. He asked the guide to show him his knot as tied with nylon, suspecting that the knot was being tied incorrectly. The guide, and indeed all the guides, were making the same mistake: they were using the improved cinch knot for the end hook but the "in line" hook was causing the line to snap at the moment of greatest pressure. The error being made was that the guides were allowing the loop to fall behind, that is to say to go on the far side of the eye. When the knot is pulled tight the line is simply cutting into itself and will snap quite readily. It is easy to make this mistake and it is the one thing you really have to watch for. Properly tied, this knot will hold almost any Spring.

Incidentally, to hold roe onto a hook you tie the knot in place a little way down the shaft of the hook which will enable you to pull a little line through the eye through which you insert the roe and then pull the line tight.

Your hook-up for plug-cut fishing is tied by using 2/0 single Eagle-Claw hooks tied in tandem about three inches apart, depending upon the size of your herring. The leader should look like this;

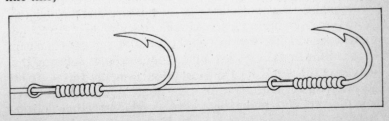

Hooking up the plug-cut herring is tricky but comes with experience. The herring must first be cut properly at a double angle. The illustration below shows the angle of the cut to the herring.

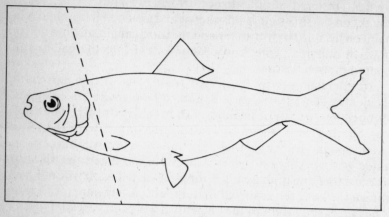

The blade must also be canted so that the cut is not at right angles, but at about forty-five degrees so that the herring looks something like this, top view;

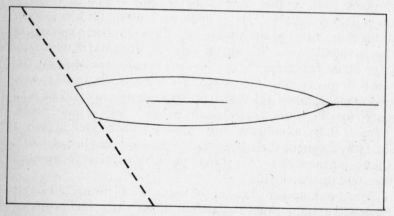

After cutting the head off with this double angle you must make a cut down the belly to remove the entrails. Then the hooks are inserted with the hook closest to the rod tip going through the body cavity at an angle, just missing the backbone. The second hook is fastened in the side in a variety of different ways and can be close to the belly or turned up so that the point is facing the dorsal fin of the plug-cut. The most popular method seems to be as shown in the next illustration. The point in having that bevel on the plug-cut is to make the bait roll over slowly; you do not want it to spin quickly, just a gradual flipping over.

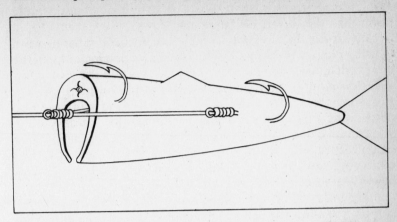

The same hook-up can be used to troll whole herring. You can mooch whole herring with your standard triple hooks by taking the hook closest to the rod tip and just passing one barb through the bottom and top jaws of the herring and then putting the second triple hook wherever you want to on the body of the herring.

To fish with plug-cut you use a six-foot leader and two ounces or more of weight - three is frequently used - and you troll this behind your boat anywhere from twenty-five to ninety feet back, seventy feet being a lucky distance for many people.

Because that herring is going to be rolling over and over, you will require a weight with a bead-chain type of swivel or simply a short piece of bead-chain which will keep your leader from knotting up due to the constant rotation of the herring.

When you have your leader ready, drop everything overboard and allow it to run alongside the boat trying different speeds and watching their effect upon your herring. When you find a speed that rolls that herring over at a rate that satisfies you, then stick to that speed. We like to see that herring making a complete circle about once every three-quarters of a second. This system of trolling with plug-cut is used in a somewhat different way at Rivers Inlet in the taking of the really big Springs. Here a heavier weight is used, generally four or six ounces, and the line goes over the side of the boat and almost straight down with just enough motion in the boat to roll the plug-cut herring over very, very slowly. The boat hardly moves at all and the line runs almost straight down into the water. Generally from forty to sixty feet is the accepted depth. This system is used not only at Rivers Inlet but also at Campbell River and generally at river mouths anywhere. The faster turning plug-cut herring is used for Coho and surface Springs, but here the speed of the boat is considerably faster than the slow trolled plug-cut.

You can see then that there are two distinct and separate ways of using plug-cut herring. The first is a fairly quick motion of the boat which turns that plug-cut quite quickly and the second is a very slow motion of the boat which barely turns the herring at all. For some reason the use of plug-cut herring can really be devastating when fishing for Coho. Sometimes, on days when you cannot catch a Coho to save your life, you can change your luck drastically by turning to plug-cut and trolling it with two ounces at a fairly fast speed which leaves the herring not very far below the surface. We generally move our boat in crescents, making little half circles as we move along and occasionally stopping to allow the bait to fall and then putting the boat back into gear lifting the plug-cut up to the surface again. It is important when you fish in this manner to note in which direction you are moving at the time you get your strike because you are going to have to repeat that direction to take another fish. The use of the crescent movement enables you to present the bait to the fish in the direction in which it is looking without having to calculate to great nicety the flow of the current. The stopping and starting takes that plug-cut herring down to the salmon if they are well below the surface and by picking up speed and raising the bait up very close to the surface, you will enable fish that are closer to the surface to spot the lure.

The whole dead herring hook-up is very seldom used when under power because the whole herring just does not react properly to a boat in motion. We very seldom mooch a whole dead herring but it is sometimes necessary when all that is available are the small frozen jack herring because you cannot cut a strip from them. If the herring are of a size which enables you to cut strips, you will find that mooching a herring strip is generally more effective than mooching the whole herring.

There is no doubt in my mind that a strip entices the salmon with its odor as well as by its appearance. Twice I have taken Spring by mooching the remains of a herring from which herring strip had been cut because we had run out of strip and there was nothing left but the skeletons and the heads and tails lying in the bait bucket. The entrails and raw flesh seem to provide a smell irresistible to the Spring.

5

Safety And Courtesy Ashore And On the Water

Some of the funniest things you will ever see while fishing happen on the dock and at your favorite mooching spot. The tales are told and re-told and, of course, lose nothing in the telling. A favorite among moochers is the fellow who carefully maneuvers his boat through the assembly of those who have already anchored using the theory, one supposes, that the center should be the best of all, then yells at his wife to let go of the anchor. His boat is nearly always brand new, the white canvas or vinyl gleaming. On three occasions now I have personally seen the little lady let the anchor go and go and go --- the captain has forgotten to attach the chain to his anchor line. The captain, now speaking in a barely audible whisper, tells his mate not to mind, to come inside; he then quietly leaves, forty dollars poorer.

A source of amusement, too, is the chap who lowers the anchor, has remembered to secure it, but has not remembered that he only bought a hundred feet of rope. His willing spouse lets that out cheerfully only to find herself holding onto the last six feet of rope with no sign of bottom and her eyes bulging with the weight of the anchor and twenty feet of quarter-inch chain. She finally lets go when she can hold no longer. As the anchor dangles ineffectually at the end of its tether, the captain makes his way to the bow, now drifting perilously close to the others. He generally slips as he dashes forward, putting him in just the right frame of mind to haul up forty pounds of dead weight in a race with time. Sometimes he succeeds in avoiding both his neighbors and a coronary but usually his boat is fended off by obliging neighbors who move their rods as he drifts by, a crimson puffing flurry of arms, festooned in rope, mumbling something about "deep, isn't it?"

This particular fellow does not usually fade into the sunset. A master of logic and circumstance, he will maneuver his boat close to shore and spend the evening catching rockcod.

Mooching is a gentle, peaceful sport which should give the participant a quiet time and space in which to enjoy the profound peace and beauty of God's creations. Respect your neighbor by anchoring a decent distance from him. Remember that you can always let out anchor line to bring your craft a little closer to the pack, but you can seldom pull yourself away from it. As you approach a group of boats, note which way they are riding at anchor which will tell you where you must lower your anchor. Remember that you will drift towards them with surprising speed as you lower the anchor. It takes time to lower an anchor; you cannot just let it go because the chain will foul the anchor rendering it incapable of grabbing the bottom with its flukes. To anchor in a 100 feet of water you must lay out at least 140 feet of anchor rope and probably 160. When the tide is really running you may need to lay out as much as 300 feet to anchor in 100 feet of water. If there is almost no tide and no wind blowing you do not need to, nor should you, anchor.

Once your anchor grabs you can pay out anchor line until you are where you want to be providing you have started off well away from the place where you wish to end up. Remember that each boat will have out a similar length of line so budget to end up elsewhere than right over another anchor line.

If your fish does foul someone's anchor line, it is up to you to pursue your own remedies. He is under no obligation to pull anchor or to help in any way. You have fouled him and it is up to you to make out as best you can without inconveniencing him. Often it is best just to break off the line as close to the anchor as you can.

If despite your best efforts, you do end up too close to somebody, then just apologize quietly and start all over again. It happens, If someone ends up right on top of you, say nothing. Just wait. Generally they will realize their error, not always immediately — usually as the wind swings them particularly close. If they do not move after a reasonable time, then you should move. Anybody who is so completely insensitive as to anchor so close will generally be little bothered or affected by anything you have to say. You will find that by starting an argument you will spoil your own fun. It is better to pull anchor yourself; after you have the anchor up you can say something gentle if you just cannot restrain yourself, but you will find that your point has already been well made.

Always start your boat before you pull anchor. If there is anything wrong with your motor it is best to find out while at anchor, not while drifting into trouble.

If you are going to be fishing with your wife or your son or daughter, one of the first things that you should do is to teach them how to operate the boat. It makes it a good deal easier to raise the anchor in a strong tide if your partner can run the boat forward as you bring in the extra anchor line. If you do run into any kind of trouble, your partner can keep the boat out of harm's way.

Further, bluntly speaking, there is no reason why you should have all of the fun. If you are going to be going out with your family on a regular basis, it is only fair that they be allowed to become involved in the enterprise. You will have lots of things to do without running the boat. By allowing them to do so, you are making them part of the adventure. They will derive a good deal more satisfaction from this than just sitting around like a fifth wheel. Remember that it will take them a time or two to learn how to dock the boat properly but that will come with a little patience. Once they have mastered the technique, then you will be in the happy position of having a fishing partner instead of being perpetually the host with a guest aboard. Remember that the correct way to leave a dock is in reverse swinging the rear of the boat out and away from the dock. You never leave a dock by traveling forward except in the rarest of circumstances.

If a sports troller catches your anchor line, which is a frequent occurrence, it is up to the sports troller to work the matter out. You are under no obligation to help him. Try not to laugh because they are frequently very sensitive. Remember to take your pliers with you, not your hook remover when you are going to lift the anchor because you will have to find the hooks and then remove them from the anchor line.

If you have an AM/FM radio aboard when you are mooching, keep the volume down; similarly your C.B. radio should be kept low. A citizen's band radio is a great item to have aboard for many reasons. The safety factor alone is worth the price but the pleasure of being able to check with others as to how the fishing is going makes the unit a real asset. You can also monitor other calls, perhaps hearing enough to tell you where the fish are. Do not overdo your use of the set — some people are constantly calling, and remember that everyone can hear you so do not wear out the microphone calling for your friend and do not use any language on the radio that you would not use in a restaurant. If the person you are calling does not answer after you have used his name twice, then forget about it for half an hour or so. Call channels are different in different areas but channel nine is generally accepted as being the call or emergency channel. After your friend answers you simply tell him to go to whatever channel you have determined is clear before you made the call. Do not choose channel eight or ten because at close distances your voice will overlap onto nine which is very annoying for others. Stay clear of channel eleven also because the commercial fishermen generally use that as a call channel. You must license your set and the forms for that will be given to you when you buy the radio. When you receive your license they will send you a pamphlet outlining the basics. Read it carefully because these sets are not toys; if they are not used properly, the government could withdraw the privilege.

When you are passing a boat always look to see if anyone is playing a fish and if they are, of course you must stay well away. When running past a group of moochers or even one boat remember to slow down until you are by. Your wake can be very annoying. Similarly in any harbor or place of anchorage where there are docks and floats or marinas, you must reduce your speed. It is really infuriating for someone who is tied to a dock to have a boat go by at high speed.

Should you be mooching when someone else's salmon runs around your fishing line or lines, do your best to free it immediately and if you cannot, then you should cut your line.

At the dock you should remember that a good number of people sleep aboard their boats and they probably did not get to bed until very late; they may not share your 6:30 a.m. enthusiasm to reach your favorite spot first and anchor before it becomes crowded. You should talk in a whisper and start your boat as quietly as possible and leave the dock as soon as you can. One morning we were sleeping aboard when a group of fellows were leaving. They made enough noise to wake the dead, but things really warmed up when something went wrong with their boat. Nearly everyone was on the dock or awake or up before the noise-makers figured out that their stern line was still tied to the dock.

Here again, whether coming or leaving the dock, there are always boats that will be bothered by your wake. It causes them to crash against the dock and spills drinks and upsets bottles and causes children to fall and generally upsets everybody. Always come and leave slowly.

If you have had a good day, share your fun. Unless you have reason to conceal the location of your success, tell those who asked where it is that you caught your fish. Tell them the depth and the method too. If someone asks you what mooching is or what the hook-ups are or how you use them, don't be in such a hurry that you will not take a moment to help them. Show them your tackle and perhaps give them one of your leaders. Under no circumstances should you ever be short with a young person. It does not make much sense to complain about the younger generation if you will not even take the time to show a boy or a girl the basics of a sport that might make the difference between them hanging around the street corner or not. Have them aboard your boat and show them your tackle and explain how it is done in as much detail as time permits. You will be making a good investment.

Be alert to the inquiries of others when you come in with a limit of fish. A gift of a fish to some tourist will mean a great deal to him. He will probably talk about it for days. Ask him how he wants it cleaned, then do it for him. On occasion we have been approached by people who wanted to know how we were catching all the fish when others were not so lucky. Aside from sharing your knowledge, such as it is, it is occasionally a nice thing to arrange to take somebody out. These people are usually there with their own boats and tackle, but things are not working for them and by taking them out and sharing your good fortune with them for an hour or two, you may be able to put them on the right track. Aside from the fact that it is the right thing to do, you may make a lifelong friend.

If you keep your boat at a dock or float, you will soon come to know the locals. Some can't fish, some are too old to do so and some no longer have a boat. The gift of a fish or a filet of lingcod given quietly is very much appreciated by these people. If you have a cabin, then remember your neighbors. If you know someone who is on a pension or of limited means, take the time to go to the house and give him a fish. It costs nothing but a little time and your thoughtfulness will be greatly appreciated.

When you are cleaning fish you will frequently find onlookers watching you or asking questions; do not be brusque, but take the time to show them if they are really interested. You may have the pleasure one day of seeing someone that you helped helping someone else. It is a nice feeling.

When ashore or afloat it is essential your eyes and ears are alive to signs of trouble. There are dozens of excellent books on boating, of course, but you will never have a chance to practice your rescue techniques if you do not see or hear the person in trouble. If you hear a "Mayday" on your C.B., drop everything to listen. Do not grab the mike as though you were the only person around. Listen to see if the Coast Guard picks up the call (highly unlikely) or somebody else who is nearer the person in distress. If nobody responds, then answer and do your best. Never ever assume everything turned out alright.

In rough weather, particularly when a calm day has suddenly turned rough, take the time to watch the small boats to see how they fare on their way back through the swells. The extra ten minutes you take to follow a car-top boat may save a couple of lives. If you find yourself ahead of one, give him a chance to follow in your wake by slowing down for him.

Watch too for people waving shirts or towels or just plain beckoning. You will be utterly amazed at what you will find. There is one hand signal which you must know and that is the hand distress signal. This consists of straight arms extended from the shoulders to form a cross then lowered to the outside of the legs, then repeated. If you see this signal, you know the boat giving it is in trouble.

There used to be a fishing camp for sports fishermen at Minstrel Island in Knight Inlet run by two of the nicest women you could ever hope to meet. A friend of mine, Frank Rosborough, and I had spent an hour or so in the store at Minstrel Island which has just about everything for the traveler. We then secured a room at the fishing camp, had supper and I then had a bath. It was Frank's turn next while I settled down in bed to read by the light of a coal-oil lamp. It was a small room and the lamp smelled, so I opened the window for some air. Carried to me just once and not at all clearly came a cry for help. It was blowing outside and it was blowing hard. I dressed as quickly as I could, made my way downstairs and out onto the porch where the cries suddenly became clearer. A call to Frank brought him out of the bathroom in his pants and tee shirt, bare feet, but ready to go. We clambered aboard the boat and used our search light which plugs into the cigarette lighter. There in the channel were two small boats, both upside down; gas tanks, life jackets, cans, oars, were spread out down the channel and drifting away at a speed that seemed impossible. We fired up the boat, cast off and headed out, keeping upwind of the two capsized boats. There was a man clinging to one, cradling a small dog under one arm, his fingers locked onto the keel. It was late September and bitterly cold and he was shaking as though he would come apart. We saw another man as we closed on them, but he was just sliding under the surface of the water as I turned the boat sideways to swing the stern at him where Frank stood ready to grab. How Frank managed to catch hold of him is beyond me, but he did.

The man was small but he was heavy with the water in his clothes and we had a difficult time getting him aboard. I grabbed him around the waist from behind, bending him over double with his head down and he spewed beer, chips and salt water all over the deck. We swung him aside when he began to cough and reached for the second man. He offered his dog first, so I took the dog while Frank wrestled the second man aboard. He was reasonably sober but his teeth were chattering so badly that it took him a moment or so to explain that there was a third man somewhere.

We flipped both the small boats over with the gaff hook in case the third man was under one of them, then took a look around with the search light. He was nowhere in sight. The search light lit up the scene like the stage of a theatre. We made a quick run to the dock where we were met by Larry Rose, the proprietor of the store. There was also a young fellow from the only fishboat at the dock and his girl. They took charge of the two men while we went back out.

We found the third man about ten feet from shore away down the channel floating face down in a deadman's float. We could not get to him because of intervening rocks so Larry Rose and the fisherman worked their way along the shore and they secured the body. Frank and I then went back to the dock and made our way along the shore to assist, but their efforts to revive the man had failed. He was where nothing could ever hurt him any more.

There was no way we could get him up the cliff to the trail on the stretcher that we had at hand so the fellows lifted him over my shoulder onto my back and with their assistance I carried him up the cliff in a fireman's hold, the other three men pushing and propping. We laid him on the stretcher, carried him to an old shed, and locked the door.

Apparently the three had left the pub at Minstrel taking a bottle of liquor with them. The two men we rescued were in one boat, the third man in the other and they were returning to their cabins across the channel. Halfway across the third man decided he wanted a pull on the bottle so he drew alongside the other boat and it was decided that he would get into their boat and they would tow his so that they could all three be together with the bottle.

In stepping from his boat to theirs the deceased had tipped both. At some point he had decided to try to swim to shore and had died of a heart attack. He stood six feet three inches and weighed 250 pounds so the double tipping of the boats is understandable. The other two men spent three days each in hospital recovering from exposure. They did not write to us directly and we never saw them again, but we received their thanks in a letter from the two women who ran the fishing camp.

That night we sat around in the kitchen of the camp, sharing a bottle of overproof rum we kept aboard the boat for emergencies. Despite the rum nobody slept well but it sure taught me a number of things I had not known before, the least of which is always to heed anything even slightly unusual which may amount to an indication that someone is in distress.

Alcohol and boats are a poor combination. If you want to have a drink, have it at the end of the day when the boat is secure at the dock for the night.

6

Birds And Herring And Things

Seagulls seldom appear at sea without cause. They are generally hungry and can tell you where the feed is located, whether it be herring or shrimp spawn or anchovies, and they can tell you how deep it is and they can tell you which way it is drifting. Seagulls and birds are not always as observant as a practiced human eye. Sometimes you will spot feed long before the birds do; knowing what to look for is half the battle.

Early in the spring, especially, you must watch for shrimp spawn. Without being too technical about it, these are small —less than half an inch in length — shrimp which appear on or near the surface of the water. They are called euphausid shrimp or "pink feed." These are difficult to see but their presence is usually disclosed by gulls of every kind hovering over them and then landing to feed. These gulls duck their heads into the water in quick pecking motions much like a busy chicken picking up grain. The gulls then rise again to hover until they spot a denser mass, then settle to pick and peck again.

As you approach you will wonder what they are feeding on because there will be no herring flipping on the surface. If you are lucky you will see little "v's" on the surface of the water; these are tiny shrimp swimming for the moment on the surface, being trapped above the surface of the water by the surface tension.

Now look about you to see which way the wind is blowing and how hard. Reading the surface of the water is not hard, but it takes a little practice. If the wind is at all strong it will take priority over the tide and move your boat in the direction it is blowing. Remember that when people say "it's a south wind" they mean it is blowing from the south. Having determined which way your boat will drift, being either tide-ridden or wind-ridden, bring it to a stop so that you will float past the gulls and not through them. If you go through them they will all fly away and your boat will disturb the shrimp or herring and you will be all alone to ponder what happened to the feed. Many a time we have fished alongside a pod of shrimp spawn only to have some fellow see us playing a salmon and then proceed to troll or drift right through the center of the swarm of gulls leaving nothing to mark the spot except perhaps a few dead shrimp flowing swiftly by or a mass of herring scales disappearing gradually into the depths.

By the way, in the water the live shrimp are invisible, or nearly so. When you catch your first Coho and cut it open, particularly in the springtime, you will have your first glimpse of euphausid shrimp. They are pink, almost red when massed together, and their little black eyes are their predominant feature. The Coho will be stuffed with them. Immature Coho tend to feed on these little shrimp in preference to herring. When very young these Coho will not take a live herring, but fishing alongside a mass of shrimp spawn is still well worth trying because the larger Coho will take your herring. The presence of this shrimp spawn in the spring is the reason that red lures work so well in the early part of the season and why those red plastic dodgers work.

More fun and more productive is a school of herring marked by gulls. Remember that the gulls are not just flying by; nor are they sitting in the water cleaning their plumage. To be feeding gulls they must be wheeling and diving and hovering and darting down, squawking and pecking. When you approach an area to fish do not just assume, because you see a large number of boats anchored in any one spot, that *that* is where you should be fishing. Use your eyes to look for a gull or bird activity of any kind. Time and time again we have seen groups of boats all anchored over a good mooching spot but by keeping our eyes open, have determined the presence of feed in another spot. By adjusting for tide and wind and making a drift by, you can often put your limit in your boat in an hour. One day we did this in the presence of about forty anchored boats and I was reaching for my C.B. radio mike to tell a friend to come over when a boat I knew placed his call. As is usual, we flipped to the channel he had mentioned, one rod still in hand with a fish on, to hear the caller say, in discussing our luck, "those S.O.B.'s could catch fish in a desert." The point is that you will greatly increase your chances of success if you keep your eyes open, look for the feed and fish next to it. Remember that this book you are reading will not do

Coho - four jumps in two seconds
Coho - a tail-walking acrobat

The early morning "bite"

Preparing for the freezer

Heart - stopping aerobatics

A large Chinook after a long battle

The no-net pickup

The bald eagle - perfection at work

Taking a look at the opposition

Two jumps in one second

Herring bag,
hose and tap

The battle is over

Yellow rockfish

A live herring with hooks in place

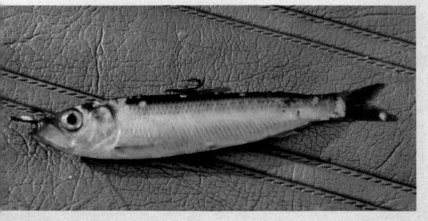

A Spring slowly tiring

Near the boat - no time for mistakes!

Gorging gulls over euphausid shrimp

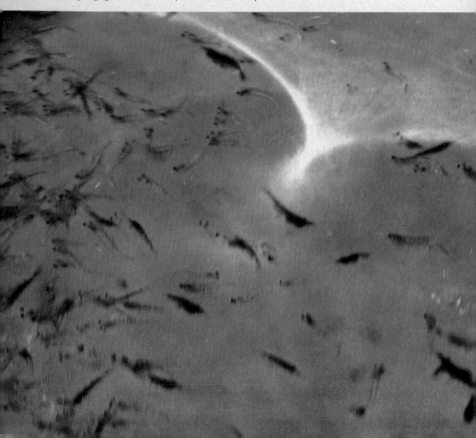

A rare picture of a euphausid shrimp shoal

A close-up of euphausid shrimp

Netting time

Journey's end

Sunrise

Sunset

half your work for you. There are fishermen who have forgotten more about herring and feed than I will ever know. You must use your imagination, ingenuity and powers of observation at all times to increase your knowledge of feed and how to find it. Talk to people, listen and learn and observe. Try new techniques. Experiment with one rod using the other for tried and true methods. Be innovative.

There are other birds, of course, which feed on herring. They are not nearly as indicative as gulls but can be of help. One surefire indicator is the pigeon guillamot - a dark bird, white patch on black wing, about the size of a hell diver (Western Grebe) but much more substantial in the neck and head. Grebes or hell divers are indicative and so are "teeterasses" (Murrelets). In all cases they must be diving, not just swimming.

There are three distinctive patterns to watch for when gulls are feeding on herring. In the first instance you will see one or perhaps two gulls hovering, generally at or near a kelp bed and therefore usually near the shore. They will be hovering above the water and darting down now and again. These gulls are following a single feeding Coho. If you can get close enough you will usually see a wake or even a fin or even the Coho itself as it mooches along the surface taking small herring or needle fish.

This is an extremely difficult fish to catch but this will be covered later.

The second situation is where a large flock of gulls is feeding by diving into the water then rising again to hover for a moment before diving once more. You will see the odd herring flipping out of the water. This is indicative of a fairly large school of herring with only the occasional herring coming to the surface.

The third situation is the herring ball - wonderful to see and much more frequent than you would imagine. Here the herring are being herded - generally by Coho although the opinion is that dogfish will herd them also. The herring have been so controlled that the center of the mass becomes compacted. This is generally an area only three or four feet square but the herring are forced above the surface and lifted right out of the water. The herring are so dense that the gulls are actually standing on them as they gorge themselves, gulping three or four or more at a time. I cannot recall ever having seen a herring ball without there being Coho present. The trick is to catch them. They are obviously at or near the surface because that is where the herring are. Seldom will they be any deeper than sixty feet. Stay well away from the ball - at least one hundred feet. Your herring does not stand a chance any closer because there is too much competition. If you stay about a hundred feet away and drift by with the tide you will stand a good chance of catching one of the Coho. Never try to anchor near a school of herring because it will soon move away from you.

Always watch for herring whenever you enter a bay; it is generally wise to make a quick spin around the bay watching for feed because as often as not the feed in a bay will not be marked by gulls. You really have to look for them very carefully. Do not just look at the water surface casually expecting perhaps a little sign to come out saying "herring here." You have to examine the surface intently as you would study a street map, carefully, intimately; seeing is not just looking with your eyes. Seeing consists of looking and thinking, examining; watching intently while consciously interpreting what your eye records. The presence of the herring may be disclosed by just one lone little flip of a tiny body against a wave Sometimes there are no herring flipping on the surface but if you will look under the surface on the shady side of the boat you will see a school or part of one moving soundlessly by. Watch, do not just look.

A little trick seldom used is to watch for tiny oil slicks on the surface of smooth water. When the herring is seized by the salmon, frequently a drop of oil escapes to rise to the surface where it will blossom, about the size of a dime, in irridescent blue and pink circles while spreading for a second and then disappearing. You know then that there are salmon feeding below. Sometimes when there are Coho feeding, you can see hundreds of herring scales drifting through the water. Head toward their source and try your luck.

Kelp beds frequently house a herring population. Make your drift past about a hundred feet away. These kelp beds generally house a population of cod and you do not want to catch those if you are salmon fishing. Sometimes you cannot see any herring, but you can feel them hitting your line. Experience will tell you when this is happening. If you want to, you can catch these herring with the use of a herring jig.

A herring jig consists of about ten tiny barbless hooks tied to a single line with short lengths of line to each hook. Each little hook has a red tuft of material at its base. The jig only costs fifty cents or so and because they tangle frequently, you should buy three or four. You may even have trouble getting the jig straightened out after removing it from the package. You must work at it slowly and pull gently and have lots of patience. A two-ounce weight is tied to the end of the jig and the other end is tied to your rod line or to a hand line.

Because the herring eat the euphausid shrimp mentioned earlier they are attracted to the little red tufts. A slight, easy upward motion of a foot or two will snag the herring, generally in the mouth, at which point you bring it in. It is not at all unusual to bring up two or three or as many as eight at a time if the school is thick. Too many at once tangles the jig. The herring are generally at about thirty feet and on down to sixty feet. If you do not get any in the first ten minutes, then you should give it up.

The guides at Campbell River use the same set-up but cast out to the edge of the kelp beds, trying for little schools of herring which are seldom visible. If the herring are really abundant it is possible to jig several bucketfuls in an evening. Unless you have a specific need for several bucketfuls you should only take enough for breakfast and perhaps a few for a friend. They are easy to clean and take only a moment to cook and are almost as tasty as trout.

Herring can also be secured by the use of a herring rake which is a long red cedar blade or paddle along the edges of which are set needle-like nails about three-eighths of an inch apart. Once the school is spotted you proceed to sweep the paddle or rake through the herring, impaling them on or in between the nails. The nail part is about six feet long and the handle the same. This system is used in areas where the herring are abundant. It takes skill, strength and luck but given the right school of herring, the system of raking can be very productive. It has the advantage of taking much smaller herring than a jig can secure for you. The nails for the paddle are hard to come by but are double pointed so you can drive them into the edge of the paddle but still have a point at the other end with which to rake the herring. A small tool comes with the nails to hold the one pointed end without damaging it while you set the nail into the wood. Watch for somebody using one then draw close to see it or ask to see it. It is primitive, but very effective.

Most people neither jig nor rake their herring, but simply buy their live herring at the resort from which they are going to fish. Not all docks or resorts carry live herring and you will have to make inquiries before setting out on your mooching trip. The coast of the mainland is well supplied, with nearly every marina having them at hand year round.

Mooching techniques using live herring or strip are exactly the same. Live herring are definitely the better bait but strip is no slouch either. The same hook-up is used for both although with the strip the top hook is frequently changed to a single hook of varying size, right from two ought down to the tiny number ten single.

If you have never cut strip, the best thing is to buy a box of pre-cut frozen strip to see what they look like. A few minutes in the salt water will thaw it out for you. Examine the shape carefully. Note how it tapers to become almost paper-thin at the tail end. To cut your own all you need is a sharp knife and a little patience. Walter Burtnick, a doctor I know, uses a scalpel and he is a joy to watch. You should cut the strip before the herring completely thaws because you will find it is much easier to work on a partially frozen herring.

As mentioned before, if the Spring are really feeding they will take just about anything. The night that I had a Spring take the carcass of a herring from which the strip had been remmoved on both sides was memorable for another reason. We had come out without a net, borrowing one each time we had a fish alongside. Three times fellow fishermen obliged, but by the time we had that last Spring alongside there was no one left in the bay and the Spring was lost because there was no way that I could get it aboard, despite various attempts.

Since that time we have learned to boat any salmon without a net thanks to a trick shown to us by Collie Peacock, a well-known guide, now deceased. There was not much he did not know about fishing. He occasionally worked at Harkley and Heywoods in Vancouver or at Woodwards in the off-season just to be doing something.

When he first told us how to boat a salmon without a net we thought he was kidding us. It was months before we actually tried the trick and found, to our surprise, that he had not been putting us on. What you do is to play the salmon until he is ready to be netted with the net that you left behind. Then you play him for about two or three minutes more. You want him dead tired and lying on his side. Once this is achieved, you lay your rod down with the tension loose right where you can grab it if anything goes wrong. Now, assuming you are right handed, take the leader in your left hand and draw the salmon gently to the surface sliding it along from right to left so that it is on its side on the surface. Now with your right hand wide open as though you were carrying a tray of beer, you slide your right hand under the salmon at the point of balance midway on the fish. Try to refrain from laughing. You now gently lift the fish up out of the water, still on its side, using the leader gently if you have missed the point of balance. You lift him out ever so slowly clear of the water and over the side of the boat then lower him to the floor where he will explode all over the place while you try to clunk him. You will be amazed that it works, but you will not be half as amazed as the people who are watching you. I have done it with a twelve-pound Spring from the deck of my twenty-foot boat which is a long way to reach. Some day when you have a fish or two in the boat, give it a try. Somebody is always leaving the net behind or dropping it overboard, so it is a handy trick to know.

The fish probably thinks he is still in the water because he is still "floating." Try not to grab him in any way or grip him with your thumb and fingers. If he slides off your hand, let him go, then try again. Just be sure to keep your fingers away from the hooks, having looked first to see where the hooks are. It is like lifting a large floating ball out of the water with one hand.

Scent upon or about your tackle is of the gravest importance. Some fellows are almost fanatical about it, some just casually careful, some do not worry about it at all, but there is no doubt that it does make a difference. Fisheries department observations and other tests have shown that Coho and Spring are highly aware of and repulsed by human scent. A salmon basically is just a bar of muscle ending in a mouth, nose and eyes. It is probable that its ability to discern, either by taste or smell, minute differences in the water leads it to its particular spawning stream. It may well "taste" its way into the right creek to spawn.

Spawning salmon will respond instantly to a foreign smell in a creek. This was first noticed by Fisheries biologists who noticed that after they had had their lunch and returned to the counting station, often there were no salmon there. Somebody figured out that after lunch some of the fellows knelt to wash their hands in the creek or to have a drink. Their human scent instantly deterred the spawning salmon from progressing up the creek.

The practical applications of this discovery are relatively simple. Wash your hands before tying your leaders and before tackling up to mooch. I usually wash my hands with a little soap and salt water before tackling up. It sounds ridiculous and looks even worse, but it seems to pay dividends when the mooching is slim.

Some of the old timers who trolled and buck-tailed used to throw the offal into a little bucket as they cut their strip. Into this bucket went their buck-tail flies to be swished around in the offal before being place overboard. Everyone was very concerned with scent. Most old timers are of the view today that scent is high on the list of priorities where mooching is concerned.

Commercial fishermen use aniseed oil on their tackle to cover up the human scent. It does not go rancid and the salmon seem to like it.

Indians, past and present, frequently put their lures outside in the rain, either on the roof of their boat or their house. This is a practice commercial tollers still use to allow the scent to dissipate in the wind and the rain. Many moochers leave their leader material in their boats for the same reason.

Certainly oil and gas are avoided by salmon. You should always wash your hands thoroughly before handling tackle when you have been handling anything greasy or oily.

Rusty hooks are of no concern to a salmon. The bottom is littered with anchors, scraps of iron, chain and cable and so he is not concerned with a little rust around the bait. But if you want to try fishing with a gasoline-soaked leader, you will wait a long time between mooches. The bad scent may eventually dissipate but it can be a long wait.

Roderick Haig-Brown conducted tests using lures as against roe. The results were staggering. Roe outdid every lure by about ten to one. Steelheaders using live ghost shrimp will tell you they are just as deadly as roe. Natural baits give off a scent which is very effective as an attractor. It stands to reason a salmon will be just as easily repulsed if the terminal tackle smells like an oil delivery truck. The salmon won't know whether to eat it or light fire to it. By the way, you will see many moochers with red-colored weights - either painted so or with reflector tape on them. This practice has been in use for a long time. It as been said that moochers used to paint their weights to look like a lure so that bystanders would mistake the weight for the lure and thereby not find out what the moochers were really doing. This may or may not be so, but red weights do help in the opinion of many. We use them. They do attract and it is not uncommon to find teeth marks on them. One day we actually had a Coho mouth the weight while we tried unsuccessfully to bring the herring up to where the Coho was, which in this case was just six inches from the surface and six feet from the boat.

Salmon are not at all bothered by engine noise or turning propellors or surface noise of any kind. You can be standing on the back of your boat yelling at the top of your lungs to a friend fifty feet away with both his and your engine going when the salmon will hit or mooch your bait.

Salmon are bothered by surface shadows and movement. Any change in the light on the surface whether caused by your shadow in still water or by the lifting of an arm or leaning over the side of the boat will alarm a salmon. It is a difficult thing to test, but may explain why one side of the boat is usually superior to the other on any given fishing day. The shady side of the boat where no shadows will be cast will be frequently the better side from which to fish. Don't laugh. Bear in mind that only about five percent of the Spring that hatch make it to the sea. Most of the ninety-five percent that do not make it fall prey to a variety of birds. Kingfishers, hawks, merganzers, grebes, loons, cormorants, herons; the list is long. Surely over the process of their evolution the salmon fry have developed defence mechanisms against this overhead danger. Surface shadows and movement foreign to the natural surface water movements must cause, if not a conscious action, at least a reflex one. A salmon in the river can definitely see through the surface and will be "spooked" by a fisherman on the bank or the movement of his rod. A good river fisherman knows this and stays well behind the salmon and keeps as low a profile as possible.

Tests have shown that the higher above the salmon a fisherman stands, the more readily he will be seen. How far below a salt-water surface a salmon must be not to be disturbed by a shadow is difficult to say but given a sunny day, I would say it would be a long way down.

Salmon are incredibly sensitive to light. One night at a little place called Glendale Cove in Knight Inlet we arrived very late to set up camp. It was September. We were trout fishing so I walked to the river's edge to look about with my flashlight. The shallows fairly exploded with spawning salmon darting in every direction, but mostly downstream into the nearby estuary and deeper water. The sudden flash of the light beam across the water had really upset them. I then placed the flashlight on a log to steady it and moved back out of its beam to see what would happen. The spawning Coho gradually returned. The light did not bother them at all and in fact they seemed to like it. The moment I picked up the flashlight the moving beam caused the same violent explosion of motion. In a moment they were nearly all gone. Wherever there was a fish left a flick of the flashlight would send it scurrying downstream.

Whenever possible you should mooch on the shady side of the bay or inlet, the salmon seem to prefer it. A salmon swimming near the boat just below the surface will, just like a steelhead, swerve away if you raise your arm or move suddenly. The boat bottom does not bother them at all and they will swim under it from one side to the other and back out again to take a bait held just two feet below the surface. If, however, you move your arm above your head for any reason the fish will be gone like a flash. Salmon like to hide under a dock or float and love the security of this. I suspect that the salmon will often come up at the herring that is in the shadow of the boat because he can take that herring without losing the protection of the boat or its shadow. This definitely would apply to baits fished fairly shallow and probably deeper if the sun is strong. You should try to stay away from the boat edge in strong sunlight and don't make a practice of leaning over the railing with your body over the edge.

Salmon are not at all bothered by the smell of their own blood and entrails as occurs when you are cleaning a salmon over the side. Nor does there seem to be much evidence to justify the opinion, often expressed, that salmon offal attracts dogfish Once after cleaning a salmon overboard we caught a dogfish with the entrails spilling from the side of his mouth but that was only once. Often you will hook a salmon or have a mooch shortly after cleaning a fish overboard.

There are so many things in nature that are unexplained. At Glendale Cove, the day after the flashlight incident, I got up early to light the fire. There in the shallow water were two huge coastal wolves fishing in the river. They would walk slowly across the stream, then grab a salmon by the back just ahead of the dorsal. They seldom, if ever, missed a fish they lunged at. The fish was then carried to shore and the portion just behind the head eaten daintily, one paw holding the fish down. The portion taken was never much bigger than a man would take biting an apple twice. Then the wolf would pick up the salmon by the head and shake it until the belly contents fell out onto the grass, roe and all. The shaking was a laborious process but each wolf persisted until the belly cavity was empty, or nearly so. Later I counted thirty-two fresh carcasses on the marsh grass in an area about the size of a dining room table. After each fish was emptied the wolf would lie in the offal, all four feet in the air and squirm and roll, twisting and turning in the slimy mess. The rolling lasted about half a minute or so and then the wolf would stand, look about him, and return to the river for another fish. I watched them for nearly two hours; the procedure never varied exept now and then they would play with each other, nipping and snapping and jumping playfully. They were male and female. At the end of their fishing they waded silently off across the river to disappear into the bush, leaving a very puzzled fisherman sitting on the shore.

I discussed this incident with Tommy Tompkins, the out-doorsman, who knows a great deal about wolves but he had never seen anything like it. He pointed out that dogs sometimes do this with strange feces, or their own, but the exact reason remains a mystery.

Sometimes you will find anchovies among your herring.

British Columbia has hundreds of thousands of tons of these little gaffers in schools off our coast. They are not harvested for a variety of reasons and sometimes, some years even frequently, schools of them can be seen along our inland shores. You can readily distinguish them in the water because they appear to have dimes glued to either side of their gill covers. You will see these little round ten-cent pieces flashing at you as you look beneath the surface of the water. The herring vendors sometimes sell them instead of herring and they are just as efficacious as herring for mooching but have one drawback, which is that they cannot be trolled and still remain alive. If you have one in your hand you will observe that the lower jaw extends forward well past the upper. In addition, their noses are much more pointed than a herring's nose. The configuration of this lower jaw causes it to be forced open if the anchovies are trolled at any speed and they expire quickly when this happens. They are in all other respects an excellent bait and indeed, are preferred by some moochers.

By the way, "jack herring" are simply herring that are smaller than the usual bait sold. Moochers have preferences in choosing their herring and a good many fishermen prefer these little jack herring over their bigger brothers. There is perhaps a tendency on the part of smaller Spring and Coho to take a small bait more readily than a larger one. However, there can be no doubt at all that a larger herring is the better bait for the larger Spring. The bigger the bait, the bigger the fish. These smaller herring are quite deadly for Coho, usually being fished with one number ten hook through the nose. Sometimes the fellows refer to these small herring as "firecrackers." By small herring is meant a herring less than three inches long, the average herring being five and a half and a big one being seven or eight inches long.

It is not unusual to jig a herring ten inches long and weighing most of a pound. Over eight inches in length they seem to lose their appeal for the average Spring.

The systems used to keep herring alive aboard the boat are various. The simplest system is a plastic garbage can sitting in the middle of your little car-topper with a scoop made from a plastic bleach bottle. The water is aerated by scooping some out and pouring in fresh. The herring are caught in the bucket either by hand or with a little dip net. Catching a live herring in a garbage can on a cold January day is sometimes annoying, so the dip net is a good investment. Don't buy a light colored bucket or garbage can; the herring don't seem to like them and swim around frantically knocking their scales off and sometimes jumping out. The herring like dark and gloomy colors.

Most tackle shops sell a double-bucket system which is a bucket with holes in it inside a bucket without holes. The inside bucket has a cute little door and fastener. The idea is to fill it with salt water, buy your herring and carry it all to the boat. Then you dash off to wherever it is you are going, pull out the inside bucket and hang it over the side where the salt water will flow through it keeping the herring alive. It has too many drawbacks to enumerate, all stemming from the fact that the buckets are too small really to be of any use.

Some rented boats have herring tanks built right into them and these are really nice to have. The owner will explain how to use them.

Most popular of all on bigger boats are the cast iron and canvas bait bags. They come in various sizes but are expensive. The bag is square, fairly deep and sits on the rear of the boat. Various systems are used to supply the fresh salt water. You may, of course, simply pour salt water in the bucket letting the surplus spill out. Most fishermen use a bilge pump. These bilge pumps can be mounted on the transom outside the boat without the use of a through-hull fitting and when the switch is thrown, the pump sucks up salt water and pumps it into the bag. It won't work when the boat is planing or running really at any speed at all because the pump and hose are lifted clear of the water. On the other hand, a through-hull fitting is a very dangerous thing and to be avoided if at all possible. If it gives out, then your boat fills with water, generally while you are away.

The bilge pump is screwed to the transom as close to the bottom of the boat as possible but as far away from the engine leg as you can put it because otherwise it will pick up the exhaust if the motor is running and this will quickly "exhaust" your herring. The hose runs up the back of the boat and tucks into the bag between the canvas top and the iron brace. The pump has two wires, one of which is run to a simple on-off switch mounted wherever you want and then runs from the on-off switch to the battery. You should buy an in-line fuse holder with a five amp fuse and splice the fuse into the line just before it reaches the battery. The other wire for the pump simply comes into the boat and is grounded by attaching it to the engine anywhere there is a bolt or screw that will take it. Most pumps will say in the instructions to attach the black wire to the negative terminal of the battery. The white one, then goes to the engine for grounding. If you wish, you can run the white one directly to the positive terminal on the battery.

Most of these bilge pumps come apart by twisting them open,

so before you install the bilge pump you should open it up and paint the little pump blades with red lead or any of the paints recommended for boat bottoms. This keeps the impellor blades free of any growth. Be sure to run the pump for a while before you put herring in the bag because the lead and/or arsenic in the paint will kill your herring almost instantly.

I have grown tired of the little bilge pumps with their plastic impellors because they last only a season or so at a cost of thirty dollars. I have now mounted a ninety dollar JABSCO pump inside the transom and have run a hose down the transom to below water level. A JABSCO pump will last as long as the boat will last, or longer. If anything goes wrong with a JABSCO impellor it can be replaced easily for a few pennies.

Some fellows put on timers to keep the herring alive all night. They are expensive and hard on your batteries and the timers don't seem to last very long. These can be handy on a long trip, but we have found that the herring generally knock off their scales during the night which makes them poor bait. Remember that you will need a cover over the bag or any container if you are leaving herring overnight. The seagulls are very early risers. If you leave a dozen herring in a garbage pail full of water overnight with no pump system generally only two or three will survive. All in all, it seems better to spend the two dollars for good fresh herring each morning. The vendors deserve the business because the service they offer is invaluable. Where we keep our boat there is a family of mink which come aboard in the dark to eat any herring we may have left in the bag and they always leave the heads in a neat little pile on the forward cushions.

One morning we came out to our little car-topper at Sechelt to find that the salt water in our garbage bucket had frozen solid from top to bottom. It had to be pounded and kicked around on the dock before the solid block of frozen salt water would come free. In weather like this it is necessary to keep your head warm at all costs because that is where most of the heat loss occurs. If your feet are cold, you are being told by them that your body, and especially your head, is not well enough protected. Don't bother with putting on an extra pair of socks, what you really need is an extra shirt and a good big toque. If your head and body are warm enough there is, believe it or not, no need even to wear gloves.

Some boaters attach a copper tube with a little elbow to the stern of their boats to pick up salt water for the herring bag as the boat runs along. This is a simple rig, very handy and it takes only an hour to install. You simply buy four or five feet of three-eighths inch copper tubing and attach an elbow at one end. You then take some copper straps, not aluminium, and clamp the tube to the stern of the boat with the elbow just peeking under the bottom of the boat so that as you run, the elbow will scoop up water forcing it up the tubing and into the bag. You clamp the tubing in a couple of places making an "s" in it or at least a curve, so that it won't turn. You run it up to the bag and you can attach a little copper tap, which is handy when you don't want water running into the bag. You can travel as far as you want and you will arrive with fresh, even happy, herring.

One word of caution: if you are going to run up to the end of some of our long inlets such as Toba or even Jervis Inlet, intending to take a good supply of herring and stay overnight to fish in the morning, remember that frequently the rivers and streams that run into these inlets leave a thick layer of fresh water on top of the salt water. Your herring, even if you have a timer or set the alarm so you can water them by hand every couple of hours, will all be dead by morning. Your pump will have picked up the fresh water instead of salt water and the herring will quickly die. It can be a disappointment on a big trip, especially if you plan to stay two or three days and bring along ten dozen herring. If you are intent upon fishing the very end of a long inlet, you are probably going to have to do it with dead hearring.

By the way, all the herring bags sold are white, which is too bad, but make sure when you buy your bucket to carry your herring from the pond to the bag, that this is dark because it will keep them from jumping out.

In summer the warm water holds very little oxygen and the herring have to have fresh salt water frequently. In the winter the icy water holds lots of oxygen and indeed, so much so that a dozen herring will sometimes make it through the night without watering. We have found that for the average session of mooching we need eight or nine herring each at an absolute minimum. If there are two of us aboard, we generally take two dozen. If there is no attendant at the pond, then you put your money in the box first, then take your herring, dipping out a bunch and pouring them quickly into your bucket, counting as you go. If you want large ones or small ones, try to dip them out individually without disturbing the whole pond. The scales come off easily. Alternatively, take a good scoop of herring and hold it just below the surface of the water while you pick out the ones you want, quickly returning the rest to the pond. Remember that the next customer wants his herring with the scales on.

7

Chinook And Coho

There are five species of Pacific salmon of which only two are really sports fish. The other three species - Sockeye, Pink, and Chum salmon are "commercial" salmon. Only rarely will they take a lure. Sometimes Pink salmon, which are sometimes called Humpback salmon, can be taken at the river's mouth using any one of a number of small, generally red, lures.

The two Pacific salmon that do take a lure are the Coho and the Chinook salmon. The word "Coho" is also correctly spelled "Cohoe". These are commonly called "silvers" by our American neighbors. Chinook salmon are called "kings" by the Americans. There are a variety of names for the Chinook salmon along our coast. They are called spring, blackmouth, smilies, and whenever over thirty pounds in weight, they are called "Tyee". The commonest appellation is "Spring." The commercial fishermen lean to the word "smilie", but apply this term only to Spring salmon over twelve pounds in weight. The name "Blackmouth" comes from the fact that their lower gums are always black as opposed to the Coho which generally have white gums. The problem in identifying a salmon by gum color is that sometimes a Coho's gums look black when you have only Coho to look at. Also Coho frequently have some black pigmentation in and around the gums that can throw you off and indeed, sometimes causes identification to be completely wrong.

There are other characteristics to look at. The tail of the Spring has spots all over, both top and bottom, while the Coho have spots generally only on the top half of the tail; the Coho tail looks silvery while the Spring's is dull. Spring have a heavy distinctive odor when brought in after a fight and tend to be slimy.

There is, however, one absolute test for species that is

irrefutably definitive. Attached to the stomach of every salmon are "caeca" which are part of the digestive tract. They look like little fingers, dozens of them, all lying in a row when you open the fish. The Spring has between 140 and 185 of these little fingers while the Coho has only 45 to 60. When you cut open your fish, after the first time you have looked at one of each, a glance will tell you which one you have caught. This is the one absolutely reliable test. Accustom yourself to tell the difference. The dock arguments become quite strained sometimes and it is nice to have someone around who really knows.

Coho are called "blueback" sometimes because of the bluish sheen on the back, but this name generally is used when the fish is small and under six pounds. Usage along the coast has reduced this arbitrary six pounds in some areas to three pounds.

You will hear the word "grilse" used from time to time but again this is just local usage. The word grilse should properly be confined to mature Atlantic salmon coming in to spawn for the first time. On our coast the word grilse is generally accepted as meaning a small Coho or Spring over twelve inches in length, which it has to be for you to keep it, but under three pounds. There may be a new regulation coming soon requiring you to leave the head and tail on any salmon under three pounds in weight so that it can be checked as to its legal length.

Coho spawn in the fall from September through to the end of November and sometimes even later. The female makes a shallow indentation in the gravel and lays about three thousand eggs. The male fertilizes them and she then covers them up with coarse gravel and they both die. The "gravel" is really small rock which allows plenty of water through to flow over the eggs as they lie under its protective covering. Once hatched the fry live a full year in the stream, descending to the ocean the following spring as they are replaced by a new hatch of fry. Coho spawn in the most unusual little creeks which appear to have almost no water. No creek that runs year-round is beneath their dignity.

Some Coho, particularly in the more northern streams, spend two years in their stream of birth but the percentage that do this is fairly small.

Most Coho then spend one or two years in the salt water and statistics today indicate that about eighty-five percent of Coho landed are in the three to three and a half year old category. At spawning time, all Coho considered, the average weight is about eight pounds as the fish enters the stream to spawn. The world's record is a thirty-two pounder taken right in Cowichan Bay on Vancouver Island. When one considers that Spring salmon spawn after three, four or five and even six years, the suspicion is that a thirty-two pound Coho is probably four and a half years old, not three and a half years old.

Every year you will hear arguments over "northern" Coho. The tell-tale sign is supposed to be a hooked nose and this Coho is generally a little bigger than others that you will catch. Fisheries research indicates that some Coho move out through Johnson Strait and through the Strait of Juan de Fuca into the waters off the west coast of Vancouver Island. These fish spend their summer months on the continental shelf and some range as far north as the Gulf of Alaska and also south well down into California. These ocean-going fish then return to spawn in the creek where they were born. They are much bigger and heartier than those which spend their lives in the Gulf of Georgia and this is the reason that they are sometimes called "northerns." The problem is that some local Coho develop a pretty fair hook on their noses too. But, if you have been taking seven and eight pound Coho regularly, then catch one weighing eleven or twelve pounds with a hooked nose you may assume that you have taken a "northern." In fact, it may have spent its last year somewhere off the coast of California or Oregon. It is somewhat difficult to form any opinion as to the ratio between the local Coho and the "northerns" because the ratio will vary depending upon where you are fishing. The northerns do not usually show up until mid August, although we have caught them in late July from time to time.

From the sport fisherman's point of view, the first reasonable Coho fishing is in the month of April, perhaps March at the earliest, when the two year old Coho grilse pester you as you try to catch the three year old Coho. At three years of age he is just getting ready to really grow; he will weigh two or three pounds but is at that time switching from the euphausid shrimp to herring for his diet. During the summer he will grow from his three pounds to twelve and on up. In these early months of April and May and the first part of June, sports trollers generally use red and pink lures behind a dodger or flasher because the Coho have been and are feeding on the reddish euphausid shrimp. The problem with trolling is that very often one has to use eight ounces of lead to take a lure down to where the Coho are. This weight, coupled to a dodger, does not lead to very much of a fight from the poor little three pound Coho. Most trollers don't even stop the boat and merely reel in the fish or lift it into the boat by hand when it comes alongside. Be that as it is, they are nice to eat fresh and they are easy to thaw from the freezer. You will not be able to mooch them until late May at which time you have to use small herring.

Most fishermen do not find Coho as interesting or exciting as the Chinook. To say this is perhaps a little unfair to the beautiful Coho whose speed and fighting tactics provide such sparkling excitement to so many but they do lose in comparison with the Spring on a number of counts, size of course being foremost. Size provides that edge of excitement which is so important to everyone. This is part of the gambler's excitement which can turn a day's fishing into a lifetime memory when you hook a really big one. When you are fishing for Spring the fish that causes your rod tip to respond could be a ten, a twenty, or a forty, even sixty, pound trophy. It can happen at any time because every fish has the potential of being the big one.

Women generally find this aspect of mooching particularly attractive. It has always surprised me that there are not more women moochers. There is nothing about mooching that requires a great deal of speed, strength or aggressiveness. Some quickness of hand and eye and a little patience and some fortitude in cold or wet weather are all that are required of a moocher and all these characteristics lie easily within a woman's province. Don't be surprised if your lady companion outfishes you, for experience indicates to me that you will have to go your best lick just to keep up with her. It is probably one of the best husband and wife sports that there is to be found anywhere. You can both then share, at the table, in the other's success.

Chinook salmon tend to prefer the larger rivers for their spawning. The female Chinook will deposit up to ten thousand eggs in an area from eight to fifteen feet long and about five feet wide which is called a "redd." In the redd are a number of pockets, sometimes as many as ten or twelve, into which she drops her eggs. The male is right alongside fertilizing as she lays; she then covers the eggs with gravel, actually with inch to inch-and a half rock, to a depth of a foot or even eighteen inches. That is quite a mass of rock, but she bumps and brushes it all in on top of the egg pocket, mainly with the use of her tail. In the pocket the eggs, a thousand or so, slip and slide between the rocks, their tough outer skin resisting the force against them as they roll, for each is laid individually, between the gaps in the rock finding space a-plenty. The eggs are washed by the river water which flows not only over the rock, but through the gaps all around the eggs and up from below and over and through. Depending upon the water temperature it takes about fifty days for the eggs to hatch. The little alevin as they are called then take about a hundred days to work their way up through the gravel during which time they live on their yolk sack. They actually live quite comfortably in the rock or gravel free from most enemies. They gradually work their way up through the gravel and into the stream. If the river has silted over they have to pick at the crust until they find an opening to allow them access to the flowing river. Heavy silting can destroy them completely. When they emerge into the stream they are about three-quarters of an inch long. Their food consists of minute organic plankton, diatoms, and other organisms.

Studies indicate that about twenty percent of these newly-hatched Chinook will spend a full year in the river, the other eighty percent head almost immediately for the ocean. The death toll in the river is staggering. Only an estimated average of three to four percent make it to the sea with the main part of the hatch succumbing to the vicissitudes of stream life. In some rivers and streams the return to the sea is as low as one percent, with the high figure being estimated at thirty-five percent. Regardless of the accuracy of the statistics, the time spent in the stream by these tiny Spring reduces their numbers drastically. Birds of every kind dine upon them almost at will, trout devour them and frequently drainage ditches lure them to their death.

Both male and female Chinook stay in the river after mating. They take about a week to die then leave their bodies to deteriorate in the river to provide food for the various life cycles expecting it. It takes little imagination to appreciate the effect of hundreds of Chinook bodies slowly deteriorating in a river, allowing their rich nutrients to escape gradually downstream to feed plant and animal alike. Since the tiny organisms feeding upon this decaying protein provide food for the tiny Chinook, it can truly be said that their life-giving parents continue to feed them long after their own deaths.

River conditions are obviously vital for a proper hatch. If the water flow slows and the level falls, the eggs will be exposed and die; if the river floods, the rush of the water frequently washes the gravel from the eggs and they are exposed and carried off to die. If the river runs at too high a level silting frequently occurs which results in the gravel being covered and the water flow over and around the eggs ceases; they suffocate. If sufficient water still reaches them and they do hatch, a thick layer of silt will often bar their exit from the gravel. It is a tough life for the little fry.

We must learn to protect our rivers and streams; to keep good wide green strips alongside our river banks thereby ensuring a slow runoff of the rain into the water courses from the logged-off areas. This applies to every little stream, every water course of any size from the one going through your own back yard to the little slough-like trickle up at Williams Lake. Every moving fresh water flow is vital. That little flow of water through the park is mother to a thousand Coho. There are fry in water courses you could step across even if you were on crutches — flows that can be destroyed by driving a bulldozer across them just once, flows that could be dispersed by using the water for just one drainage ditch.

Those Chinook that do reach the salt water may travel a thousand miles ranging up the coast as far as Alaska or they may stay within a hundred miles of their own river of birth. In the sea their enemies are, of course, legion. They are preyed upon by everything; cod, sea bass, birds, man; all take a share of the river's bounty such that on the average just two survive from the hatch to return to their river to start the cycle again. This percentage return to the river must gradually improve if we are to continue to enjoy these magnificent fish. There is little we can do about the Chinook once they reach the ocean save to return, when caught, the smaller ones. The obvious place to do our caretaking is in the rivers and the streams. The most effective and least artificial of improvements in this area seems to be the artificial spawning channel which is simply the creation in the river or stream of an area containing the correct size of gravel with a controlled, steady flow of water guaranteeing the right temperature and the proper rate of flow at the proper level to enable the eggs to hatch. This system seems to interfere with nature the least of all of the techniques. It enables the fish normally resident in that particular water course to reproduce and for the usual laws governing survival of the fittest and natural selection to operate upon the hatch. It also provides any one river or stream with a wide variation in size so that the Chinook are not all of a uniform size which is frequently the case in a hatchery.

The usual return to the spawning grounds for Chinook occurs when they attain four years of age or, if they have spent a year in the river before going to sea, as five year old fish. Some fish do not spawn until they are six or seven year old salmon and this is particularly true of the northern rivers such as the Yukon River where nearly all young Chinook spend a year or more in the river and return to spawn at age six or seven.

These older fish are really something. The world's record, caught commercially, is up around one hundred and twenty-five pounds. At Rivers Inlet it is common to catch them weight sixty pounds and similarly, Campbell River produces big ones, forty pounds being not at all unusual. In fact, most places in and around Georgia Strait can and do produce forty pound Chinook. You can expect only occasional encounters with Springs of this size. The usual "big one" weighs around twenty pounds and is a four year old salmon. Fisheries records recently tallied indicate that roughly half the sport-caught Chinooks are two years old, another third are three years old, ten percent are four years old and the remaining seven percent are grilse or really big ones. Statistics vary and will continue to do so as research methods are refined and there remains a great deal that we do not know yet or understand.

A phenomenon you will frequently encounter is the "jack spring." Nature wants to ensure the eggs of a female are fertilized. Certain male Spring, generally two year old fish, reach maturity in this time; their milt or "dry roe" as it is sometimes called, develops. They turn dusky along the sides and bottom just like a mature spawning Spring and enter the sea stream or river along with fully mature four and five year old Chinook. They are therefore available to fertilize the female. You will catch these young males while mooching. They are not as pretty as the other Chinook but are, of course perfectly healthy fish. It is a mistake to call any small Spring a "jack" because the term "jackspring" applies, or should apply, only to the precocious male with fully-developed milt, ready to spawn. With a little practice he is easily recognized.

The word "Spring" is a bit of a mystery. (Most Spring salmon spawn in the fall although there is a spring spawn also.) Perhaps spawning patterns have changed over the years, but one fact is clear and without dispute; there is good Spring mooching in the ocean every month of the year. I suspect that there are Spring salmon entering the rivers to spawn every month of the year, also.

What a sight these big Spring are when seen in a river. One evening we were trout fishing in the Kitimat River when a friend's two young children called my attention to what they thought was a shark in the river, upstream from where we were angling. What a sight it was. It was a huge Spring salmon. The world's record sports-caught Chinook came out of a nearby river a few years later and weighed ninety-two pounds. It is hard to estimate the weight of a fish by sight but this certainly would have been in excess of fifty pounds. It took a golf-tee spoon on the first cast, moving sideways about twenty feet in order to do so. When she hit that spoon, it nearly tore the rod out of my hands, taking out fifty yards of line in its first little run, knowing that something was wrong, but not knowing what. It then proceeded to show me who was boss, moving at will through the river until my twenty-pound line was down to a few turns on the spindle despite the fact that I had walked out over the top of my waders into the icy September river. At about this time it decided to come back downstream, giving me just enough time to gain some line and lose my footing. As I floated downstream, I continued to reel, groping for the bottom with my wader-clad feet. The fish swam much better than I although we both ended up against a log jam of sorts. I went under, the water holding me against the logs and it was only youth and luck which enabled me to climb up from under the water, my head finally surfacing in a plume of white water. As I groped to secure my footing to lift myself out of the water, the fish snapped my rod off two feet from the tip when the rod brushed against a log for a moment. The children were laughing so hard, they told me afterwards, that they had tears in their eyes. It was a long wet walk home, but an experience never to be forgotten.

In the salt water, a twenty-pound Spring can and will take six hundred feet of line from a reel in one long, uninterrupted run. He can snap a rod off clean if it touches the edge of the boat when he's sounding under it. A blistered palm from trying to slow the reel down is not an unusual experience.

One day we hooked a twenty-two pound male Spring off Epsom Point on Thormanby Island. There were so many boats around we started up the motor to follow it as it ran to clear ourselves from any possible interference. We followed that fish for forty minutes at seven knots with the rod bent almost double. It took us another forty minutes to bring it to the net. As it was being laid to rest, a silver beauty, in the fish compartment, someone pointed out it was derby day for one of the local derbies at Pender Harbour. We had tickets somewhere, found them, and my partner took second prize, a floater jacket and a sleeping bag. That fish deserved some sort of special recognition. You can land most any Coho in fifteen minutes, most Spring in twenty, but occasionally you will hit a real dandy.

Another memorable day my partner had two Springs in the boat and had lost another after a long fight. The two in the boat were twenty-five pounds and twenty-eight pounds. Yours truly had not had so much as a nibble. My partner then hooked another big one and this one stayed close to the boat, sounding, as they sometimes do. I brought my herring up to twenty-five feet to avoid having the lines tangle and as luck would have it, my turn came. The salmon took the herring, went under the boat and took out five or six hundred feet of line in one long, screaming run. Then it sulked, away out from the boat, giving me time to maneuver my rod around the propellor to play him from the side of the boat closest to him. He came toward me slowly, brooding, moving his head slowly from side to side. It wasn't until he was about fifty feet from the boat that I realized something was wrong. He was there, but not fighting. Suddenly a large rockcod broke the surface, twisting in the current. You can well imagine how surprised I was. There was no way a rockcod would have taken my herring at a depth of twenty-five feet in one hundred and twenty feet of water and then run full speed for about six hundred feet. It wasn't until we got him aboard the boat that the answer came. The Spring had been hooked by the bottom hook, the one at the end of the line. As he tore along the bottom, he scared up the rockcod, catching it in the back as it darted out. The Spring had, of course, then broken the line between the two hooks, probably at the same moment the cod was snagged. The Chinook then continued on his way, leaving me to reel in the rockcod, expecting a big run at any moment. Oh yes, my partner's third fish was a nice even thirty pounds, a Tyee.

8

Feeding Habits: Coho Vs. Chinook

There is relatively little that has been said about the differences in feeding habits between Coho and Chinook and yet an appreciation of these differences is absolutely essential if one wishes to mooch effectively. The two species differ in their feeding habits and are as dissimilar in these habits as, say, cod and perch. Once appreciated, these differences will open to you an entirely new field of methods and will dictate your techniques as well as greatly increasing your chances of success. The methods of fishing for each species differ vastly, something that has never really been grasped by most fishermen.

The ideas set forth in this chapter are theories only, but are based on observation and tempered by experience. Repetitive and even intense observation has its limitations in salt-water angling because the observation is severely limited. Only rarely will you ever see a Spring take your bait, perhaps never. Coho are somewhat more frequently observed, but sightings are still rare. There are, however, definite and distinct differences in the method each of these species employs to secure its feed. The differences will some day be fully understood but for now we can only theorize. My theories are based upon personal observation and inquiry, but they are not completely definitive. Rather, they are ideas to be tested, analzysed, added to, tempered and refined.

Coho are highly aggressive, competitive and greedy in their feeding habits. When raised in a tank the Coho require segregation if they are to survive because all the food supplies are "requisitioned" by the aggressive few, leaving the weaker to succumb. The same does not hold true for Chinook, who under the same conditions all survive, for they feed casually and without the aggression displayed by the Coho.

The reasons for this difference in behavior are probably complex. With all Coho fry spending a year in their stream of bith, and that stream generally being a small one, it may be that food is scarce, indeed it probably is scarce, so that competition and aggression become necessary as an adjunct to survival. It is known that for some reason a large number of Coho fry slide downstream to the estuary almost as soon as they are hatched. In the estuary, the mortality rate is high with some biologists suggesting that the transition from fresh to salt water is not easily made in that early stage of their development.

The aggression may also stem in part from the fact that the Coho life cycle is at least a year shorter than the Chinook life cycle. Perhaps the aggression is needed to ensure a rapid weight gain to maturity.

The Chinook pyloric Caeca may provide a clue. Food enters each salmon's stomach and is subjected to acids that reduce it to fluid form whereupon it enters the pyloric Caeca much as our food enters our small intestine to travel through our bowels and eventually to be eliminated. Most of the nutrients are extracted in the bowel. The Chinook's "bowel" contains roughly three times the digestive bowel present in the Coho. Perhaps this more highly developed digestive process enables the Spring to extract more of the nutrients from the food than the Coho is able to extract.

My observations indicate that a Coho, even amidst plenty, as when engaging a large school of herring, will eat frantically. He usually approaches the school of herring from the rear or slightly from the side near the rear, sliding smoothly forward into the school to match its speed which is never much faster than two or three miles an hour. He then opens his mouth wide and bites gently into the herring where they are thickest, engulfing four or five or more herring in a single mouthful. He then slows or turns aside, swallowing greedily those he has captured. He does not masticate them and they reach his stomach almost untouched. He then pauses, turning sometimes to look for herring that have fallen from his mouth - a frequent occurrence. If he sees one he will pick it off quickly as though afraid to lose it to another Coho. He then leisurely returns to the rear of the school to repeat the process. This technique holds true for schools of larger herring, but here the Coho concentrates on one single herring, nearly always grasping it by the tail and then gobbling forward although he frequently loses the herring and will turn to snap at it, taking it down head first once it has been disabled. If he sees a single herring he will maneuver at full speed to take it from the tail, but if impractical will seize it anywhere to crush it, juggle it and finally gulp it down. When in competition with other Coho he will frequently miss it altogether because of his excitement. Two Coho will occasionally hit the same herring at the same time; neither has any objection to turning and swallowing any portion of herring falling free when torn asunder. If one Coho has only the head of a herring in his mouth with the rest hanging free while he is trying to swallow it, his fellow Coho will frequently charge him and tear all or part of the herring from his mouth.

Salmon do not have a reverse gear; they cannot back up to take another run at a wounded herring and so must make a circle and come at it again. Because of the motion of the tide and the fact that the herring is falling, they frequently lose sight of it. I am almost positive that their eyes do not see anything below the level of their own nose. They frequently appear to take no notice at all of herring that are just below an imaginary line running the length of their body. In their haste to seize a new herring, they will simply keep going and not bother to turn back for the missed herring. If in competition with other Coho, this does not hold true and they will turn and fight to obtain the missed herring.

Given the time and interest you will yourself see some aspect of Coho feeding not here revealed. Coho are much more likely to be observed than Chinook for Coho are generally surface feeders. I have actually observed each of the phenonena described here and some of the behavior I have observed on a number of occasions. The accuracy of the description may be verified to some extent by examining the stomach contents of the Coho that you catch. When cleaning a salmon you simply squeeze the stomach from the lower end and the contents are forced from the end of the stomach nearest the mouth and you will be able to see something of what he has eaten and how he has eaten it. I have done this to over two thousand salmon, a conservative estimate, to see what could be learned. I have found shiners, shrimp, herring, anchovies and needle fish in their stomachs and by studying the herring swallowed by the salmon have learned something of *how* the herring are swallowed. It was at one time thought that salmon always took the herring down head first, but this is not the case. Coho nearly always swallow the herring tail first.

Confirmation of the fact that Coho take three and four small herring at a time can be found by looking at the stomach contents to see the herring packed together just like sardines in a can with one bite mark covering three or four.

The Coho has another feeding pattern altogether which consists of moseying along the surface, so close to the surface that his back raises a wake and the dorsal is sometimes visible. He is moving along the surface picking off small herring swimming right on the surface. His progress is frequently marked by a single seagull hovering above him, trying to pick off disabled herring missed by the feeding Coho. The seagull sometimes actually touches the wave crest with its feet as it hovers above the Coho. This feeding pattern can be observed only in very calm water, but is particularly prevalent among Coho feeding near or in kelp beds. The progress of the Coho is slow, slower than a man walking, and this causes the seagull to have to really work to hover above the Coho, which it does only with difficulty. Exactly the same pattern can be observed when you next play a salmon with seagulls about. If you take a moment to force the salmon to the surface until its back causes the water surface to crest, almost immediately a gull will swing over to hover above the salmon as it moves along just under the surface. The gull is not trying to get the salmon, it is just imitating its feeding pattern, thinking it has found a feeding Coho. The Coho does not mind the gull or try to evade it in any way; the two will continue to fish together until the Coho sinks beneath the surface for a while, usually to surface and repeat the process.

Coho that are feeding in this manner can be caught by power mooching or by casting a lure directly in front of him. You can cast your whole live herring or strip or use a buzz bomb. Power mooching will be covered in a later chapter.

Herring have an interesting schooling instinct which I have observed; as the school moves along, the lead herring which are in front on top of the school drop down to the bottom of the school and slide along gradually to take their place at the bottom rear of the school where they are most vulnerable to attack. They then gradually work forward and up to the front top again. It is a trait passed on from generation to generation because it is observable in schools of herring just hatched as well in mature schools. It is almost as though the system were designed to spread the danger evenly throughout the school because it is generally the rear of the school which sustains the heaviest losses.

This surface feeding pattern for Coho is not exclusive to the Coho; Spring do much the same thing, but only occasionally will their backs cause the surface to swirl. The feeding Coho raises a crest on the water almost continuously.

Spring salmon are supposed by many to be deep feeders but this is simply not a fact. The presence or absence of feed dictates to the largest extent the depth at which the Spring will feed.

The pattern of feeding for the Spring is not at all similar to the

Coho's. To my certain knowledge Spring deliberately thrash through herring to stun them, then turn to feed on the cripples. I don't think that the Coho thrash a school of herring. They do feed in among them and they will herd them and circle them and they will follow behind another Coho to pick up what he leaves, but they don't thrash or barge the herring.

The Spring, on the other hand, barges his way through the school then circles to pick off those that are stunned. Sometimes a Coho, because of its aggressiveness, will reach the stunned herring before the Spring does, but it's the Spring that does the thrashing, not the Coho. This might explain why the Spring "take" is so delicate and careful as opposed to the Coho's frantic pulling at the bait.

To see a Spring salmon thrash a school of herring is a rare, awe-inspiring, sight, seldom seen but once seen, never forgotten. It will awaken in you the realization that these magnificent fish really have to work hard for their feed.

The Spring will sometimes hit a single herring with the object of stunning it so that he can return to eat it. Moochers often experience a single hit on their line and then moments later the Spring will mooch the bait. If your hooks are sharp enough you will sometimes catch the Spring when he hits your single herring.

When thrashing a school, the Spring starts from the bottom of the school driving up and whipping his body as a man would whip a handsaw. His rush ends when he bursts through the school at which time he circles and sinks to pick up those he has killed, stunned or otherwise maimed. His mouth is shut tight for this thrashing with no thought of grabbing a herring on the way through the school. I have observed this thrashing clearly on two occasions, both early in the spring; the salmon were clearly recognizeable as large Springs, both because of their huge size and because there just weren't any Coho that big around. On the second occasion when I observed the thrashing, I set my two rods, one at thirty feet and the other at forty-five feet. There were four big Springs that I could see thrashing and I was so excited that my fingers were trembling. Something bumped my herring hard, really hard, then nothing. Quickly I stripped off six feet of line, leaving the rod in the holder, trying to simulate a stunned herring dropping to the bottom. Sure enough, my line went completely slack but not until a good long minute and a half had passed after the initial bump. So much time had elapsed that I was actually reaching for the rod to strip off another ten feet or so when he took. Moochers are continually amazed at how long it can take for a Spring to finally take a bait. I grabbed my rod, set my feet and reeled as fast as possible; he was there for a split second but before he could be struck, he let go. The herring was badly slashed on both sides where it had been pulled from his mouth. I threw it back over to lower it to forty-five feet again but before it reached that depth the line again went slack. This time the frantic reeling paid off; the rod bent double and I hit him, driving in both sets of hooks, as it proved later. The salmon was plainly visible to me at the moment the hooks were set; he had paused in his upward journey to shake his head, trying to free it of the weight of the sinker or perhaps because my reeling had taken the weight of the sinker away from him as my line caught up to the sinker so that he though he was free. The moment my hooks set he raced the last few feet to the surface and scooted along the surface at top speed, his dorsal showing. He seemed to be still trying to outrun the weight as I gave him absolutely slack line without even my ratchet on to see what he would do. He weighed an even seventeen pounds.

Spring often take advantage of feeding Coho, frequently cruising about below them. The Coho is a notoriously untidy eater. When he turns aside with his mouth full of herring he frequently drops several. Given sixty or seventy Coho doing the same thing, a Spring has very good reason to prowl below them. He has equally good reason to prowl below feeding Chinook. Generally he stays well below them and takes the herring one at a time, daintily and carefully, seeming almost to test it by biting or squeezing it before finally swallowing.

There is no doubt that a Chinook frequently "tries" a herring and rejects it. The Coho may miss one herring or lose it or see another one closer, but seldom just reject it. I have actually seen Spring, good big Spring, take the bait. They seldom bother to bump a single herring, but come up at it from underneath and behind to seize it gently, ever so gently, in their jaws cross-wise just behind the head and just ahead of the dorsal or just on it. This is their ideal "'take." Unfortunately I have never seen what happens next because the moment the Spring feels the weight on the line, he is off.

Moochers argue for hours as to what it is that alarms the Chinook. Does he feel the hooks? Does the feel of the leader material alarm him? Does the sight of either of the hooks or the leader alarm him? Well, experiments with leaders have indicated to me that sometimes the color of the leader can put off the mooch to some extent. Your leader should as closely as possible match the green-blue of the salt water. Its thickness does not seem to matter save that very heavy leader material will impair your live herring's ability to move through the water. The feel of the leader by the Spring as he takes the herring does not seem to alarm him in the least. Why should it? He cheerfully munches prawn, shrimp and ghost shrimps, all three of which are prickly, heavily shelled and horny. Sure, he knows a herring shouldn't be hard, but he is not alarmed when it is, at least not in my experience. Similarly, he is not panicked by the hooks unless he makes a very direct contact as he sometimes will on a head mooch. It is no easy thing for a salmon to maneuver his length into the exact position to secure a frantically swimming herring. Frequently he will miss the herring altogether or just nab the tail; when he lets go to secure a better grip it sometimes escapes him; sometimes his course of travel is a little fast as he comes up on his tangent and he takes the herring by the head. When this occurs he usually encounters the lead hook and he will try to disengage or, if it doesn't bother him, he will open his mouth wider and take the herring right down.

It is my opinion that the main cause of a Spring not completing his mooch is the fact that the herring is attached to the weight and this is the main source of alarm for the Spring. It is for this reason that the Spring keeps swimming up with the bait - he is trying to get away from the weight because it is unnatural and completely alarming to him. The herring, in his senses, should be free and not attached to something which seems heavier as he swims away from it for he is now pulling a long loop of line.

He is not at this point hooked or even slightly in contact with the hooks. When you catch up with him you will frequently pull the herring and hooks right out of his mouth.

Conversely, when he has accepted your herring, taken it down head or tail first, all the way down, and it is irretrievably hooked, he will frequently still rise straight up, causing your rod and line to go slack. He rises because he is in trouble, something has gone wrong and he knows that extra weight shouldn't be there and he is trying to escape from it.

He does not rise if you set your hooks in him as he mooches it at ninety feet — he runs or sulks or shakes his head the point is that when he's in trouble, real trouble, he'll fight. When he's bothered or alarmed, he rises rapidly. He does not rise because he has taken the herring from below and wants to keep rising. If so, then most Spring mooches would result in your line going slack; in fact the phenomenon occurs only in about thirty percent of your mooches — those mooches where he has been upset by the weight attached to the herring.

If rising to the surface were his natural way of feeding, he would do it in a much higher percentage of mooches. It has been suggested that Chinook, happy to prowl near the bottom, want to test these stunned or wounded herring that they encounter for freshness and so mouth the herring. This does not seem an adequate explanation considering their keen sense of smell. It seems to me that the mooch must be characteristic of the Spring because he stuns or kills the herring first and hence has no need to grab at it. He takes his prey quietly, knowing that it is incapacitated.

You must realize that a Spring can take a single swimming herring just as slick as a whistle. The herring need not be stunned. Spring also strike a trolled bait with tremendous speed and accuracy; they are more accurate, I suspect, than the Coho. Not many people realize that Spring are just as much surface feeders as are Coho. I did not realize how frequently they will take on the surface until an episode off Sunset Marina about two miles north of Horseshoe Bay. We had been having poor success and my partner suggested that we try over by a little point just north of Sunset. We left our mooching tackle in the water and I started rowing over to the point. I did not then have an outboard. Being young and in good spirits though somewhat bored by the inactivity I really stretched myself out, rowing just as quickly as I could. We had not gone a hundred feet when the first Spring struck. In two hours we had six Spring in the boat and I had a blister on my bottom the size of a fifty cent piece. They would only take when I was moving the boat just as hard as I could row it. We returned night after night through late July and into August, frequently catching our limit, using the same method each time. I solved the problem of the blister by sitting on a lifejacket. We learned to lighten up on our weights, using just an ounce, and we also learned that the height of the rod tip above the water is critical.

These are surface-feeding Springs looking for herring in the top four inches of water so if your bait is below them, they are going to go hungry and so are you. The bait has to be right up near the surface, just below it, and no deeper than three or four inches. This was the reason we only took them on the very fast troll for only then would the herring be just below the surface. Exactly the same technique applies for surface-feeding Coho. I discovered the fact that the height of the rod tip above the water makes a difference when my partner was some nine fish ahead of me. It occurred to me that the only difference between her tackle and mine was that my rod tip, because of my rod holder, was two feet higher above the water than hers. The rush of the water was lifting my partner's line closer to the surface than it was my line because my line didn't strike the surface until much farther back thereby forcing my weight and bait fractionally lower in the water. This may at first thought seem to be such a trifling difference as to be inconsequential but bear in mind that we were using the same rods, same reels, lines, weights, leaders and herring. In fact, I was baiting both leaders with the live herring which were in a bucket behind me. It became very annoying to be always one and sometimes two fish down. When it occurred evening after evening the rod tips finally came to mind. A slight adjustment to the rod holder resulted in an immediate and lasting change. We also found we could let out as little as twenty feet and still have the Spring hit the bait. Forty-five feet proved to be ideal. Sometimes at seventy feet our herring skipped on the surface.

Fishermen who fish bucktail fly use exactly the same technique. Every now and again you will spot a couple of men who are real "pro's" with special holders mounted on the stern which keep their rod tips about eighteen inches above the surface. Incidentally, live herring trolled in this manner with an ounce or an ounce-and-a-half of weight are much more effective than a bucktail fly.

To return to our Spring; unless someone is very fortunate or uses a television camera, the mystery of what a Chinook does with the bait after his initial contact is probably going to remain a mystery. We know he often abandons the bait after the first contact. We know he may be alarmed by the weight or the hooks or the leader or perhaps by the scent. I have ruled out the scent because I don't think he would take it in the first place if he didn't like the smell of it. It has been suggested that he contacts the herring for the purpose of killing it and then lets it go in order to turn it to take it down head first, but the examination of stomach contents indicate that he will take it down either way. Indeed he nearly always swallows small herring tail first. One thing is sure and that is if it is being mooched and not trolled, thereby appearing to be in trouble, the Spring's first contact with it is usually very delicate. Sometimes he does not even leave teeth marks. At times the teeth marks can only be seen under the most careful scrutiny. The Chinook seizes it, then releases it almost unharmed. This indicates to me that he cannot see the hooks but may be bothered by them when taking the herring in his mouth. My experiments with leader indicate that it is definitely not the size of the leader so in my mind, that reduces it to one of two factors; it is either the hooks that he feels or he is bothered by the fact that the herring is attached to something, in other words the weight. It may be both of these factors. If you use small enough hooks - say number tens or twelves, your chances of having the Spring swallow the herring seem to increase. This would argue for the hooks being the main factor. On the other hand, experimentation has shown me that if you use a lighter weight your chances of successfully hooking him greatly increase. The problem is you can't use too light a weight because of the current. Something that is not too widely known is that if you use a lighter line, that is to say, reduce your main line to eight or ten-pound test, you are able to use lighter weights because the current doesn't sweep the line to the surface so readily. For this reason some moochers mooch with a ten-pound test main line. I have found this to be unsatisfactory because I lose so many fish. Perhaps I'm not delicate enough. I've used number tens and number twelves quite often , but the problem with these is that often you get a mooch and you react to the mooch by reeling in, but there isn't enough "bite" to the hooks and you miss the mooch. With the small hooks the distance between the barb and the shank is so small that the hook frequently doesn't set into the fish's jaw but simply pulls free. People who use these very small hooks seem to be the cocktail fishermen who simply throw their lines overboard and have a drink while hoping that the fish swallows the whole show.

There are, in fairness, many fine moochers who do use small hooks. They use hooks as small as number twelves and they fish successfully. A strong argument, of course, can be made out for using number tens and number twelves when fishing for Coho with a very small herring. The treble hook is simply inserted in the nose and with the small herring anything bigger than a number ten is going to seriously impede its motion.

The technique for striking the mooch when using a small hook is completely different than when fishing with a number six hook. The moocher using the small hook simply waits out the mooch and lets the Spring swallow the herring before striking it. When he sees his rod tip go slack, he simply leaves it alone for perhaps as much as half a minute before gently reeling up to it and then striking it. The problem here is that as often as not he will travel with the herring and decide to let it go. The moocher then misses his chance to strike the salmon while he is carrying the herring.

It seems to me that the Spring rises with the herring just as readily with number twelve hooks as he does with number sixes and if this is the case, then he is not bothered by the hooks, but by the attachment of the herring and hooks to the weight. Another fact that argues for the weight being the decisive factor is that the herring are frequently mooched just nicely between the two hooks in the live herring and the teethmarks indicate that he dropped the herring without ever having touched either of the two hooks. I think he has dropped it because of its attachment to the weight. This would mean that the most effective system of all for mooching live herring would be the use of a very light line so that you could then use a very light weight. I have compromised with a fifteen-pound test and generally use a two-ounce weight. I think you have to stay with number six hooks in the main to have a decent chance to hook the salmon on the "mooch."

On the dock at Monteray in California a sports fisherman explained to me a system which they use very effectively. They use a pyramid-type sinker and a large swivel. The pyramid sinker is slipped onto the main line and then the large swivel is tied on which is large enough to prevent the pyramid sinker from sliding over it. The leader is then tied to the swivel leaving the pyramid sinker to slide loose on the main line. As the line is lowered over the side, the weight slides down to the swivel and this is lowered to the bottom and then slack line is fed slowly which allows the herring to swim free just as far as it wants from the weight which is resting on the bottom. This allows the salmon to mooch the herring with a long distance between the weight and the herring and indeed, he can travel with the herring if you allow that main line to slide through as he takes the bait.

I have tried the system but all that it ever brought me was rockcod - probably because we have so many compared to the area where this fisherman fishes at Monterey.

He went on to explain that the first indication of a bite comes when the rod tip, which is slack because the weight is lying on the bottom, suddenly dips when the Spring lifts the weight off the bottom as he moves away with the herring. I keep promising myself to give it another try in an area which is heavily fished and which would therefore not have the problem of the rockcod. It is a system which would certainly avoid the Chinook feeling any weight when he pulls on the herring. Perhaps you might give it a try.

Sometimes when your rod tip goes slack you will reel up fifty feet of line only to feel nothing except your weight when you stop to check. What has happened is that you have overtaken the Spring, relieved him of the weight which has bothered him and he coincidentally has arrested his upward rush just as you stop reeling. Be alert, for your rod tip will again suddenly go slack as he starts to rise again or it will pull down if he decides to drop. A good way to test this is, if there appears to be nothing below save your weight and bait when you stop reeling, simply strip off ten feet or so; you will be amazed to find how frequently your rod tip again goes slack. You must then return to reeling in your line as quickly as possible. Sometimes of course the spring has simply let go of the herring, not being hooked.

One day we hit a run of Chinook in Quarry Bay on Nelson Island. It was early March and as events were to prove later, these fish were from a Vancouver Island hatchery. We put seven in the boat on a beautiful Friday afternoon - not a cloud in the sky nor a wave upon the water. We were new to the wonders of the citizen's band radio and being proud of our catch, for it had been slim fishing in the whole area during the preceding week, we proceeded to tell a friend about our good fortune. Well, the news sure reached a good number of ears and probably lost nothing in the telling because the next morning when we nosed into Quarry Bay, having slept in, there were thirty-one boats in the Bay. It was embarrassing because as we swung into the mouth of the Quarry, three or four of them gave us a toot on their horns. We try to keep a fairly low profile when we mooch but had not realized how poor the fishing had been nor how frequently people listen in on the C.B. Part of the reason for the tooting was that nobody had taken a fish up to the time we arrived; they were relieved to see us arrive to give proof to our claim of the previous day. It is not unknown for a boat to claim its fish came from Quarry Bay when actually they were caught at Thormanby Island.

Well, we fished as hard as ever we could because of course we were anxious to prove that there were Chinooks there. Whenever the wind permitted, we drift mooched but because of the mass of boats, we had to choose a drift right at the mouth of the bay, that is to say, much further out than we normally would fish. At our furthest point out of the bay that day we were in one hundred and eighty feet of water and our drift would bring us in to a hundred feet before we had to start our engine to move back out to avoid the other boats. The tide came and went, but we did not have so much as a slashed herring for our efforts and neither did anybody else. We were debating whether or not to leave, it being almost noon, when my line went completely slack in one hundred and sixty feet of water. We watch our lines carefully in drifting over an inclining bottom so I had just checked my line by bringing it up twenty-five feet. I knew that I was not resting on bottom.

I grabbed for the rod and reeled up as quickly as I could. In the quiet of that little bay my reel sounded like it was hooked up to a microphone; I stopped about halfway up, was amazed to see my line was still slack, then continued to reel just as hard as my aching forearm would let me. My rod finally arched over and I could see the salmon below me about twenty feet down in the clear green depths as I struck it. That salmon had come up over a hundred feet in one clean rising motion before my line had caught up with it. It gave me a real feeling of satisfaction for had I not stayed at it, there would have never been a strike. It was a fine hard fight, then fourteen pounds of silver resting in the fish hatch, the only fish caught there that morning, sorry to say.

It is because of this type of a mooch that I have dwelt at such length on the importance at understanding of the Chinooks' feeding habits.

In time most of the mystery will succumb to man's incredibly inquisitive mind as tidbits of information are gathered to gradually paint in the mosaic of the mooch. I hope the things I have observed and set out here will contribute to the puzzle; of course I may have misread the information and be confusing the true picture. Probably the truth will lie somewhere in between. Regardless, we must start somewhere if only to posit theories which can later be debunked in the light of keener observation and additional experience. Even given full knowledge of the salmon's habits, the sportsman will have to work for his fish, only out-guessing the prey occasionally, thereby making the quarry worthy of the name and of the game.

9

Mooching Techniques Generally

In an earlier chapter you learned the moocher's knot. Having it at your fingertips will enable you to tie any type of leader you wish. Some prefer a single hook in the nose or at the top of the strip and a treble hook in the dorsal or at the bottom end of the strip. That single can be almost any size that pleases you from the big single two/ought down to a single number ten. Some fellows tie two number ten singles for strip, burying all but the point as they insert the points from the flesh side, the theory being that the salmon will inhale the whole strip before realizing it conceals two tiny hooks. Some prefer a single hook through the nose of their live herring because they feel it swims better. They are also aware that sometimes the herring is mooched on the head and they do not want to alarm the salmon. Some moochers use a triple number six in the nose and a single number two in the side of the herring which, incidentally, is very hard to place.

Some put the second hook in the belly down by the anal fin. The logic of this placement appeals to me, but after lengthy testing of this hook placement I have discarded it. It just hasn't worked. It seems so logical but for some reason it has not worked for me . It may be that the fish feels the line running between the nose hook down the side of the herring to the anal fin or it may be that after his initial bite, after he has bitten then let the herring go, he feels that second hook as he starts to take the herring from the tail end. A mooching salmon most often takes the bait from the tail end because the head of the herring is away from him as the herring tries to get away, so perhaps he feels that hook in the anal fin and lets go.

One hook-up that must be mentioned and which has proven to be very effective is the use of a single number one hook when mooching with strip. The strip is cut in the ordinary manner save that the head end of it is pointed like an arrow rather than being cut on the diagonal; the number one hook is then simply inserted from the flesh side up in the point of the arrow. The Spring or Coho is allowed to take the bait and given plenty of time to swallow it. The effectiveness of this type of hook-up indicates once again how frequently the Spring like to take their bait from the tail end. By the time he gets to the single number one hook, he has most of the bait already down his throat. Of all the hook-ups for mooching strip, I find this to be my favorite.

If you are going out mooching for the first time you probably do not know anybody who mooches so you should get Mike Cramond's book *Fishing Holes of the West*. This book will tell you exactly where to mooch and what spots are best for mooching and how to mooch them.

The problem of *when* to mooch is complex. As to the time of the year, there are Chinooks for the catching year-round and here it is suggested that you read your local paper for their advice as to the current hot spots.

Opinions as to what time of day to fish are varied. There can be no doubt that the early morning and the late evening are the most productive times regardless of the tides. I personally have always felt that the most productive time of any day is from sunrise to 10:00 a.m. This holds true for both Coho and Spring. Coho in particular like to feed in the early morning light and when they are scarce, really scarce, early morning is sometimes the only time of day when you can catch them. Similarly, Chinook fishing early in the morning is vastly superior to any other time of the day, save perhaps just at sunset through until dark.

For years I have been puzzled as to why fishing would fall off in the very good weather. It seemed to me that when the skies were clear and sunny the Coho were reluctant to bite and the thought crossed my mind that they didn't like the strong sunlight. Finally Bill and Dort Abbott from Pender Harbour put me on the right track. They were of the opinion that on cloudless nights when there was a moon shining, the Coho fed all through the night. The idea seemed a little far-fetched to me, but subsequent investigation has borne out their opinion to a near certainty. Commercial trollers catch salmon all through the night when the moon is shining and although I haven't had an opportunity to fish extensively at night, I have caught both Coho and Spring in the light of the full moon. It is well known that you can catch both Coho and Spring off any well-lit dock in the dead of night. I fully intend to experiment with the moonlight salmon mooching in days to come, but in the meantime I have confirmed that almost without fail the Coho fishing is much poorer after an evening when the moon has been shining brightly. The matter bears further study, but at the present time, this would seem to be the fact.

Fishing for either Coho or Spring on a pitch black night when there is no moon is a complete waste of time. I have fished perhaps twenty or twenty-five times in the pitch black of night to see if anything would take, but I have never caught a fish save when I have been fishing near a dock with lights. The mooch most definitely dies as it grows dark.

Why are the early morning and late evening the best times for mooching? It seems that all of God's creatures need to have a little shut-eye and fish are no exception. Jacques Cousteau is of the opinion that fish sleep, or some of them anyway. My years of river fishing indicate that while salmon may not sleep in the sense of lying on their side, they most definitely require periods of rest and you can see them off in the back-eddy of a pool or lying in quiet water.

A salmon has to eat to support himself. Assuming that he has to rest, which is not too far-fetched an assumption, then he would most likely rest in the dark hours when feed is more difficult to find. His eye works much like our eye, and he has to have light in order to see. No doubt his digestive system continues to function on an involuntary basis as does a human being's and therefore he is hungry when the first light of dawn appears. This is why the morning mooching is so good. He might then spend his day in search of food depending upon its abundance and combine that with traveling in the direction that he wants to go. He may be sweeping up the coast looking for richer feed and colder waters or he may be returning to his river of origin.

As the day draws to a close his natural instincts will tell him that he has to spend a quiet time during the night when he won't be traveling and he won't be feeding and the same instinct will probably tell him it would be wise to have a snack before going to bed and I think this is what makes the late evening mooch so good. The herring at this time of day are all traveling as vigorously as possible towards a protected bay or point or the lee side of a shoal to have a quiet place to spend the night without battling the current. We have seen them time after time just at sunset swimming for the lee of various points and into little bays. The Spring are aware of this habit and generally take advantage of the herring's ritual to have their evening meal.

Early morning and late evening aside, there is no doubt that there is an increase in feeding at tide change whether it be at high tide or low. Again, Jacques Cousteau has observed this feeding frenzy among many species of bottom fish, always at tide change. Perhaps the salmon takes advantage of the reduced water flow to look about, perhaps the herring are momentarily confused; whatever it is, tide change does make a difference. My personal feeling is that the change of tide makes a difference not because the salmon feel that they should feed at tide change, but because the change of direction of the water flow makes the spot where you are fishing a completely different place to fish.

Suppose for the moment that you were fishing in the Squamish River and at any given moment the river reversed its course. All of a sudden you would be reversing your whole fishing technique to bring your lure into the water that flows in the lee of the large boulders. I think that exactly the same thing happens in the ocean. Given a large number of boats fishing the drop-off on a shoal and with fishing very poor, the change of the tide will reverse the entire picture. Suddenly an area which was not a sensible place for a fish to lie becomes exactly the right spot for him to lie. He may make his adjustment by sweeping across the shoal and taking shelter in the lee of the shoal where you have been fishing for a couple of hours without success. Suddenly, on a change of tide the fishing improves and the instinct is for one to say that the fish started to feed on the change of the tide. I don't think this is so at all. I think that very often people fish in stupid places because the spot was good the day before or last week or the last time that they were in the area. They arrive there to fish the tide change and will do well either before the tide changes or after the tide changes but seldom at both times.

There are certain places on certain shoals and points which are good regardless of tide and these places are what I call "travel" areas. The fish lie in these spots when the tide is flowing in a certain direction because it tends to sweep feed to them. When the tide changes, the spot is no longer good to lie in because the tide is flowing the wrong way, but the spot continues to be good fishing because it happens to be in a channel or at a place where the salmon habitually travel in order to arrive at a destination. This particular theory needs further investigation but frequently I have noticed a change in the character of the fish that we have caught in these "travel" areas as the tide changes. Coming up to the tide change the fish, say, will be Jacksprings and Coho which are lying in that particular spot because the feed is swept to them. On the tide change, they disappear, traveling over to the other side of the shoal looking for greener pastures. The particular spot may remain very good fishing, however, because of the traveling Springs going by on their way to their spawning grounds. The character of the fishing changes because the Coho and small Springs are no longer present but all of a sudden you find that you are catching large mature male and female Spring which are obviously just about to enter a river. This has happened to us so often on the tide change that these travel routes are beginning to make an impression on my thinking.

You must stop to characterize the place where you are going to fish before you fish it. Figuring out the flow of the current is not always easy, particularly if there is a wind blowing. If you drop your lines over and watch which way the current sweeps them or look in the water to see which way the algae are drifting or perhaps drop a peanut or a bottle cap overboard to see which way it is swept, you will have your answer. Having ascertained the flow of the current, think about the place where you are going to fish. Does it provide a lee for the salmon? If not, why are you fishing it? If it is known to you as a good travel spot, then fish it allowing for the direction in which the salmon will be coming. If it is not a good travel spot and is not a good lee spot, then you shouldn't be there even if there are thirty boats sitting there. Remember that people invariably will anchor at or near a boat that is already fishing a spot even if it is the wrong spot. Use your head to tell you where to fish.

Having outlined with some certainty the periods of time that I feel are good for fishing, I must confess that if the fish are there you can catch them at any time of the day or evening. Coho in particular seem to feed all day and when I've had a late evening and sleep through the morning mooch, I will frequently try for Coho in the late morning with reasonable success. If there are no Coho about, then I most often just skip the afternoon fishing and go out about 4:00 in the afternoon to fish through until dark. If fishing in an area has been poor, I do not bother to fish the middle hours of the day regardless of the tide change.

However if fishing is good Spring can be taken at any time whether it be high noon or otherwise. There is a very popular misconception as to Chinook being near the surface early in the morning and late at night. The feeling for years has been that Chinook don't like the light; that only in the first light and in the last light of the day do they venture near the surface.

This is a complete fallacy. You can and will take Spring right on the very surface or at twenty to sixty feet at high noon on the hottest day of the year. The mistake probably came about because Chinook fishing is better at the two extremes of day;

people have hooked them at forty feet and assume that they were only at this surface level because of the semi-darkness. In fact you can take Springs at that depth all through the day. Try a line at forty-five feet or sixty feet wherever you are and you will be pleasantly surprised.

One day we had taken some youngsters out to try for salmon to enter in the local derby. It was just a tiny derby with hidden weights and little prizes donated by the local merchants. We fished from 6:00 a.m. right through until noon without so much as putting a fish in the boat. We tried every spot we could think of. You can well imagine our disappointment. We came back into the dock tired and disappointed only to find two more youngsters eager to have us take them out and give them a chance at the derby. I was particularly tired and declined to take them, but my partner insisted that we should make an effort, so after a quick bite to eat we decided to give it a whirl. There were still a couple of spots we hadn't tried. Drift mooching is a lot of work because you have to put the boat into gear and bring it back into the current and take it upstream to allow yourself to drift back over the spot. I was so darned played out that I simply took us to what I though might be a good spot, considering the tide, and threw the anchor out. Right then occurred one of those strange things that happen from time to time. The kids were both anxious to have a rod in the water and as I was stripping out for one of them I was so pressed by the other that I simply stopped at forty-five feet and put the first rod in the holder, designating it for one of the kids. I proceeded to tackle up the second rod and was about to put it over - it was in my mind to put all of the rods down to the bottom and then up twenty-five feet because that was the type of spot we were fishing - when the first rod doubled over with the weight of a twenty-two pound doe Chinook. We put eight big Chinook in the boat, all over ten pounds and three of them over seventeen pounds, in just under two hours. Not one Spring took at any depth deeper than sixty feet and most of them took at forty-five feet. We were in one hundred and forty feet of water. Now, if we had fished the bottom, which was the usual technique when at this spot, we would have all been without a fish. The reason I can say this with certainty is that I was so busy that I put my own rod right down to the bottom and left it there while I baited and netted fish for the others. It didn't have so much as a single mooch in the whole two hours and I released my live herring unscathed.

The question of course arises as to how you are to know when the Spring are at forty-five feet. Well the first thing is that if you can see herring on the surface, that is probably the right depth to fish, but secondly there is a trick to it.

When Chinook thrash a school of feed the stunned ones drop in an erratic motion. This erratic motion is copied by the action of the famous buzz-bomb lure. You can do pretty well the same thing with your live herring by stripping it out three feet at a time but very slowly. In this manner you can accurately imitate the appearance of a stunned or crippled herring falling slowly to the bottom.

When you start to mooch a spot, strip out the first twenty-five feet reasonably quickly. Having your line then at twenty-five feet, leave it there for a few minutes and then slowly strip out your line three feet at a time for the next forty feet, allowing about five seconds between each pull off the reel. Make stops at forty, fifty and sixty feet for about a minute. Your herring, as it is pulled down by the weight, is the most perfect lure yet devised. It is far more effective than when it is just swimming around and around your weight or dangling from it if you are using strip or whole dead herring. If you don't hit something in that first sixty feet after trying this trick a few times, you may safely assume the fish are deeper.

Frequently when you are fishing with a group of boats a new arrival will come, put lines over and immediately have a fish on. He isn't any better or luckier than anyone else, he has just had descending bait working for him.

There is no single thing you will do or can do while you are mooching that is more effective than this slow lowering of your bait. Time and time again it has brought fish into our boat when others were catching nothing. Springs, if feeding near the surface, are most likely to hit within the first sixty feet; Coho generally feed in the top sixty feet; treat that first sixty feet as though anything can happen at any moment. Remember that your first hint of a mooch will be when your line goes slack so be prepared to reel in quickly and make your strike.

I would say that if your chances of catching a salmon are two out of ten using a live herring that you can increase those chances to five out of ten by using this system.

Just outside Northwest Bay on Vancouver Island are the Ballenas Islands. Back in the days when Gordon and Sheila Blunt ran the marina, we used to launch our Springbok cartopper there and mosey around the bay and around Mistaken Island and the Ballenas. There was generally feed everywhere and Coho everywhere. The schools of herring were raked by the locals who kept the best of them alive in a bucket. It was there we first saw a system of "strip-casting" that really produced. We were mooching whole dead jack herring about four inches long which we bought frozen because we had no herring rake and didn't know anything about jigging herring. Besides we were not doing badly. The locals were cutting the heads off their freshly-raked herring and inserting a single number two-ought hook in from the stomach side and out through the dorsal side - something I had never seen before. They would then strip off sixty feet of line into the bottom of the boat. Their "cast" consisted of raising their herring clear of the water and throwing it about ten feet from the boat. It looked to me to be a pretty sloppy sort of a cast for strip-casting. They then slowly lowered the bait by stripping line off the floor, their left hand letting it slip through the right hand which also held the rod. They were picking up their Coho as they let the line out, not as they stripped it in. If they didn't pick one up on the way down, they then stripped it back in as one does in the usual method of strip-casting. We began to do the same thing with our jack herring in which we had inseted our two number ten hooks, nose and dorsal. It didn't take long to connect with the fish and the concept.

The same concept should be applied to the other end of the spectrum too so that as you approach bottom, you should slow down as you strip the line from your reel and let it descend slowly all through that bottom sixty feet of water. After you have hit bottom, bring it up twenty-five or thirty feet, put your rod in the holder and watch the tip. If you don't have a mooch in ten minutes, bring it up twenty-five feet and strip off slowly all the way to the bottom again. The trick is to work that bait with a falling motion.

Another reason for the forty-five to sixty foot success factor is that there is frequently a "thermocline" - a layer of warmer or colder water, frequently less salty, and sometimes dirty, that extends from the ocean surface down about forty feet. Skin divers are familiar with it. Very often these thermoclines are found at or near river mouths. Salmon often prowl just beneath it as though it were the surface. Frequently a bait dangled just below that thermocline can be very effective.

There is another way to accomplish your falling bait technique and that is to employ the system that is basic to the small rowboat moocher. Simply let out your sixty feet of line, then put the boat into gear and run forward until the lines are on the surface. Then stop and let the bait slowly fall to the vertical or until they fall as far as they are going to fall considering the tide and wind, then start up the motor again and repeat the process.

As a result of the Ballenas Island "strip-casting" observation, the experiences at Sunset Beach, the frequency of success in stripping out slowly and finally the absolutely deadly stop-start troll-mooch system, we were being gradually driven to realize that two factors were becoming paramount. These are the falling bait technique and the first sixty feet of water rule. These factors cannot be ignored and if you are to mooch successfully, you must remember them.

10

Troll-Mooching

Remember those gull-marked surface-feeding Coho we couldn't catch? Those surface-feeding Springs? There is a very effective system for catching these fish which often produces fish when all other systems fail. It's called troll-mooching. We have even used troll-mooching to locate the salmon and then mooched at the spot where we have found them.

If you have leaders available with the two hooks a little further apart than usual, you should use them or perhaps even tie up a special leader because you will want that second hook well back on your herring; the strikes that you will be getting will come from the rear.

Two ounces is the maximum weight you will want here; you may want to go as light as one-half an ounce. I found the ideal weight to be an ounce and a half. In troll-mooching the trick is to have your bait as close to the surface as possible without having it break the surface. Your speed is therefore important because the faster you go, the closer to the surface will be your bait, yet you mustn't go too quickly or it will break the surface. A good system is to throw your herring overboard, put your boat in gear and choose a speed that makes your herring look good in the water. It should be tracking right behind your weight and with lots of action on the tail. Again, if you go too quickly it will force his mouth open and he will quickly die. If you go too slowly, your line will be too deep.

What you are looking for here are surface-feeding fish; they are found sometimes in the strangest places. The first and best place to troll-mooch is on the top of a shoal where the water is shallow, say from thirty to sixty feet deep just before the drop-off. Similarly along the shorelines or sandbanks of shallow depth and of course along the drop-offs and always at or near any shrimp spawn that you see or a herring school. Ideal too are areas near kelp beds and alongside docks and breakwaters, log booms and in the lee of points. Each of these is the troll-moocher's special premise. If you are fishing three rods, then put out twenty-five feet of line on the one in the centre of the boat above the engine and one of the side rods should be put at sixty feet and the third one at ninety. You want the one with twenty-five or thirty feet out to be in the center of the slipstream of the propellor because for some reason the fish are attracted to that slipstream and like to come right up behind the source of it. I have often wanted to try fishing with a stainless steel propellor so that I could have the benefit of the flashing blades, but have never got around to this. I have seen boats with strips of silver adhesive strapped to the blades to give a flashing effect, but I have not tested this myself. The fellows who use it say that it helps.

As mentioned previously, the height of the rod tip above the water has an effect upon the depth of your herring. It is not as critical in a motor-powered boat as it is in one that is rowed because by increasing your speed I am sure that the herring will come a little closer to the surface. Also the length of line that you have out will affect the height of the herring below the surface — the more line you have out, the closer to the surface your herring will be. This is because of the action of the water pushing against the line and tending to lift it. With your lines out as above, you should troll in little crescents, swinging gradually to the left and then gradually to the right and stopping from time to time to allow your baits to settle to the perpendicular. This gives you that dropping action that is so effective. When you do hit a fish, take note of which rod took it so that you know the correct distance to adjust for the other rods and, of course, stop your boat immediately leaving the other two baits to settle in the water because where you hit the one, there are quite probably others. Remember that they will be attracted by the one that you are playing. If it is going to take a while to land the one that you have on, then after the other two rods have settled to the perpendicular, set them each at thirty feet because that is the proper depth for you to take a fish which is attracted to the one that you are playing.

We often just sit and mooch at the spot where we have hit one troll-mooching and it is certainly worth giving it a try at that spot. If you don't hit anything within a reasonable time, then go back to looking for them with the troll-mooch.

Try cutting directly into shore from time to time and rounding inside the points and going straight out from the points. Try to visualize the slope of the shore underwater to pick a spot where there is a lee considering the direction of the current. If there are boats anchored over certain spots that are good fishing, then move alongside them stopping to let your bait sink right alongside the anchored boats. The baits will descend like wounded herring, falling erratically at different speeds because of the different lengths of line out. When you start your boat again, they will rise to the surface as though coming to life.

Watch for kelp beds and troll the edges just as close as you dare remembering that there will be a line of kelp you cannot see if the tide is anything but dead low. If you stop alongside the kelp bed, do so at a distance in excess of forty or fifty feet or you will catch the little kelp cod and rockcod. There are nearly always lingcod in or near the kelp beds and you may want to try to pick up one of those in any event. There is no minimum size for lingcod, but unless they weigh over four pounds, they really should be returned to the water because it is a shame to destroy such a beautiful game fish when it is so small.

A four-pound lingcod is about sixteen inches long. The closed season changes from year to year so you must ask the local marina operator. The usual closure is from November 1 to the end of February. The catch limit is three fish per person per day.

If there are steep bluffs in the area, troll right up against them, as close as thirty feet. Sometimes if the Coho are small early in the season you may want to put ninety feet of line out because they are shy and don't often come as close to the boat as they do later in the season. In July and August you will find that the herring you trail twenty-five feet behind the boat in the propellor wash is very often highly effective. At Horseshoe Bay ferry terminal where the ferries hold themselves against the dock by leaving their engines in gear, they cause a tumultuous wake and the moochers move right into that wake and along its edge. These fellows frequently tag a salmon right in the heart of the morning ferry wake. It might be because the wash lifts up bottom matter but more likely it is because it catches herring and kills and stuns them. It doesn't take a salmon long to learn where to find the feed and of course, propellor-driven boats have been around for a long time. There is no doubt at all that salmon are attracted to the wake of a boat.

If you are interested in lingcod, pick a spot where the shore is rocky and sloping. You will not often hit salmon, but lingcod will rise as much as sixty feet to take a single falling bait so here you can stop and let your bait fall to within about forty feet of the bottom then start up again without risk of being bothered by a rockcod.

When you do hit a fish you should note your direction of travel because you may want to duplicate that direction of travel in order to take another.

Troll-mooching the edges of shrimp pods and herring schools is very effective, but here you should stop and start frequently. You might try letting your bait fall almost to the perpendicular, raising them just a little way and then allowing them to fall again.

One thing you have to watch for is your bait coming to the surface where it will bounce along in plain view; the next thing you know is that you will be playing a seagull. Very embarrassing. Don't panic, just play him in gently until you have him aboard. If you have gloves, put them on because while they will not draw blood, they can give a surprisingly sharp peck. If you have no glove, then distract him by waving one hand in front of him then gently taking hold of his head and neck from the rear with the other. Another system is to hold him against the floor by the body where the wings join then grab a wing tip and pull the wing across his line of vision. He will grab his own wing tip and hold it in his beak enabling you then to use two hands to free the hooks. We have never had one actually swallow a hook, usually the hook is in the beak and is easily removed. After you've released him, pick him up and gently throw him overboard. He will be as mad as hell, but otherwise, unharmed; remember that the poor bird is not exactly enjoying the experience so resist the temptation to pet him or examine him while you have him aboard.

Sometimes when you are mooching in a bay you will be troubled by "hell divers" — Western Grebes. They will take your bait just like a Chinook; here again you must distract him until you can grab him. The moment you have him he will generally calm down, making little attempt to get away, unlike the seagull. Usually he is lassooed, not hooked and it is but a moment's work to undo the hooks. They are a beautiful bird and the body is startlingly warm to the touch. They are, however, slow learners -we caught the same little gaffer three times in one day.

Do not ever simply cut the line leaving the bird to die a slow death. We have seen a few such gulls and it is not a pretty sight. Removing the hooks is like anything else, easy, after you've done it once. These Grebes will take your herring as deep as one hundred and fifty feet. You can identify their interference with your bait by the scissor-like marks on the body of the herring. The bill does not cut the herring, it just leaves a little impression like a dull pair of scissors would.

One day when we went to get herring at a courtesy box we found a Great Blue Heron tangled in the mesh of the net protecting the herring pond. We debated what to do for they are very large birds with an eight-inch pointed bill. Finally by distracting it I managed to take hold of its head from the rear, tucking its huge body and wings under my arm. Having thus secured him I was able to take a look at him, and what a beautiful surprise he gave me. The coloration on these dull-looking birds is incredible. They have orange on the leading edge of the wing and on their upper thighs and a beautiful black crest emerges from the white head with huge golden eyes. Another black crest hangs from his neck onto his chest. He gave my thumb a pretty good pinch until I learned to hold his beak apart out at the end where he had no leverage. He was so badly tangled that I had to use my knife to cut him loose but it was well worth the effort to see him fly gracefully away, tired but free.

Another time we freed a Northwestern Crow but he was so tired that when I threw him in the air he nose-dived into the freezing water. We picked him, or her, up and took it to the cabin inside my partner's jacket and there we fed it a spoonful of brandy and water which immediately improved both its health and disposition, enabling it to return to nature a little plastered, but otherwise healthy. It was so cold that morning that there was ice on the surface of the salt water. It was probably a case of there being a little fresh water on the surface from small streams but it had frozen so solid that it broke against the bow of our little car-topper as we moved through it, leaving a ragged path behind the boat as though we were some great ice breaker. We took five beautiful Spring that morning fishing in the harbor mouth despite the fact that the crow had detoured us, causing us to be considerably later than we would have liked.

Troll-mooching has the disadvantage that you must suffer the noise of your engine, but it does work when other systems fail and frequently it is of great assistance in locating the salmon, particularly the Coho when mooching is slow.

Trolling a plug-cut herring is tricky business. Your herring must be cut at just the right angle to give it that slow roll in the water which imitates a newly-stunned herring. You want it to roll over slowly, not spin like a propellor. It matters not that it doesn't roll all the time as long as it rolls most of the time.

A system of plug-cut mooching not yet mentioned is to mooch your herring in the tide-rip, like the ones at Active Pass and Cape Mudge and Stuart Island. Here again a heavy weight is required to get it down and keep it down. The trick is to lower it while in calm water then edge over to the boiling current, allowing it to be rolled over by the current down deep. The depth here varies depending upon the area fished. At Stuart Island the guides like to fish with the bait right down on the bottom. At Rivers Inlet the favorite depth is somewhere between forty and eighty feet and their trolling is done right up against the big steep bluffs. The guides at Campbell River frequently set the hooks when they see a strike by accelerating the boat away from the fish which has roughly the same effect as grabbing the rod and reeling in quickly. With novices aboard they prefer to judge the mooch themselves and set the hooks this way.

Fresh herring stay on your hooks much better than frozen for plug-cut mooching. Your hooks should be number two-ought up to number four-ought and they have to be razor sharp. Not all hooks will sharpen up properly so you should discard those that don't hone to a perfect point. Anything less than this and you might as well try to lasso them. This is particularly true if you are mooching Rivers Inlet style where the Spring will move up on the slowly-moving bait and just very delicately mouth it. Here again you must carefully judge the right moment to reel up and strike; you should wait until the rod tip is depressed and stays depressed and then make your move by reeling as fast as you can and setting the hooks when the rod arches over to the fish.

A good trick with any bait, but particularly with plug-cut herring is to take your boat up-tide from the area you wish to fish, say the edge of the shoal or a hot spot off a point. Set your baits at the depths you want, then allow your boat to drift into the spot. The current will sweep your baits into the spot ahead of your boat giving the appearance of a herring losing ground against the current, drifting tail first into the lie you wish to fish. This is one of the reasons why drift-mooching is so effective. Even if the boat sweeps in ahead of the bait it still presents a herring running with the tide as though injured or confused.

One memorable afternoon we approached a group of moochers, good fishermen fishing a hot spot off Thormanby Island. We had a guest aboard and had been mooching for about an hour, without success, just drifting down the side of the island. The C.B. radio told us that the anchored boats were hitting only the occasional salmon. We started the engine and trolled our live herring over to the nearest boat, a fellow well known to us and a fine moocher. As we drew near him we cut the motor to chat with him. All three rods exploded before we could so much as say "Hi." We netted two of the three right under his nose, much to his chagrin, but fun for us. We circled upstream and repeated the process taking our limit of sparkling Coho inside an hour, during which time he caught just the one salmon. Our depth sounder showed us that he was anchored on the shoal, about a hundred feet from the drop-off, fishing in ninety feet of water. We were taking the fish right on the drop-off in a hundred and twenty-five feet of water. It was a really sunny day and perhaps the Coho were reluctant to come up onto the shoal, but instead were schooled just below the lip, rising to the bait, then returning to the safety of the deeper water. Perhaps the herring were in the deeper water because of the warmth of the surface water but the point is that by anchoring you severely restrict yourself. Unless the fish come to you, it will be poor mooching unless you have managed to put your boat right over one of those "travel" spots.

On some days those same Coho will sweep across the shoal in search of food moving into water that is barely fifteen feet deep. It may be the presence of feed that does it, but I have a suspicion it has a great deal to do with the water temperature. The ability of salt water to hold oxygen is directly related to its temperature. In the summer two dozen herring in our herring bag will require fresh water every fifteen minutes whereas in the winter they will last an hour or more under the same conditions. It seems to be reasonable to suggest that the herring for sure and probably the salmon would prefer the oxygen-laden colder water. There are places off Thormanby where the bottom water is forced up from the depths so that even on the warmest days the surface water is quite cold. These are good spots to fish.

At Sargents Bay, called Northwest Bay by the locals, off Redroofs Road on the Sechelt Peninsula there is some magnificent evening mooching to be enjoyed, year round. When there was a southwest wind blowing and an incoming tide the water temperature in the summer months rose until it was like bath water. On these evenings mooching was hopeless. Really all you needed to do was to dip your hand in the water and feel the water temperature to know that there wouldn't be anything in the bay that night. The wind and tide were combining to bring all the warm surface water into the bay. We noted that not only were there no salmon in the bay on these evenings, but neither were there any herring.

While flying to Powell River on business one day the plane I was in passed the mouth of a fair-sized river flowing into Jervis Inlet. I was looking out the window and noted that lying against the shore on the south side of the river mouth were eight large Springs plainly visible from the air. It was October and no doubt they were waiting for the rains to come and make the river navigable. I nearly fell out of the plane looking at them, much to the amusement of the pilot. On the way back three days later, the eight salmon were still visible, but now they were lying on the north side of the river mouth. At Porpoise Bay where these planes land to pick up passengers and collect fares, I took a moment to check a tide chart lying on the counter. It showed that the salmon on both days were facing into the tide at the time that I had flown over them. Incidentally, I found it interesting that there was an even number of Chinook and found in that some support for my theory that the salmon pair up in the salt chuck long before they reach the river. If there were any Jack springs present, they were not visible from where I was. The fish that I saw were lying in about thirty feet of water or less because the bottom was clearly visible from the air. Their large size unmistakeably indicated they were Spring salmon. I noted that there was enough water coming out of the river mouth for them to have gone into it if they wanted to but obviously they were waiting for really high water before entering the stream. They were not lying right near the fresh water flow but were instead lying considerably down from the river mouth in salt water.

11

Some Of The Finer Points

It is wise to read your local paper to keep in touch with the better fishing areas. It is also handy to be able to phone a friend who has been fishing in that area to see how things are doing. When you arrive there you should inquire of the marina operator and ask at the herring pond. Ask the fellow across from you at the restaurant - ask anyone who will talk to you. Make a point of walking along the docks and inquire from fellow boaters. Ask the man who is cleaning his fish, but make a point of asking him when there are not a dozen other fellows standing around. Inquire of any charter boat operator and perhaps ask his guests how the fishing was and where they were fishing if they were lucky. Be polite but be curious.

You must check your tides and imprint the high and low figures clearly on your mind and rise or drop between the high and low tide so that you will know which way the tide is running and how fast. Think about the places you have in mind to fish and how they will be in that type of a tide. Remember that salmon, even in the ocean, generally like the shade. Remember that if a place is going to be crowded you will either have to get there early or take the less advantageous spots. Getting there early is more fun and more profitable. Make sure you have herring bucket, a bucket to pour water into that, anchor and line, lots of gas, your tackle box, knife and pliers.

If you want to have a completely haywire day with everything going wrong and no fun and if you want to avoid the many pleasure of the sea and all she has to offer, be sure to get absolutely plastered the night before you go out. Go to bed late, have no breakfast and bring nothing with you to eat on the boat. Don't take time to make coffee for the thermos, leave your camera in the room and all of your cigarettes, save two, on the kitchen table; forget to bring change for the herring pond and leave your sunglasses at home in your raincoat pocket. You will have the kind of a day you won't forget, or enjoy.

Seriously, the pleasures of mooching, whether or not you catch a fish, have so much to offer that it is a shame to waste your time on the water with a hangover. Besides, don't laugh, it will have a definite effect on your fishing performance. Once you are really mooching even a cold will put you off. Try to get up early, really early. Have a look at the weather and enjoy a leisurely breakfast, bring a thermos of coffee, some sandwiches, your smokes, lighter, sunglasses, and camera.

There are eagles nearly everywhere along our coast and these magnificent birds enjoy mooching from the moochers. We try to release our rockcod unharmed, but if there is an eagle nearby, you should pick a medium-sized cod and smack it with your fish club. Then throw it well away from the boat to catch the eagle's attention. The eagle will descend in a beautiful series of maneuvers, snatch the cod from the surface of the water, then fly with it to its nest or perhaps just to the shore where it will serve as lunch. If the eagles are really hungry they will come as close as ten feet from the boat; the trick is to photograph them as they hit the cod. It is very hard to do. The eagles have a system of talking to each other that is fascinating. They modulate their cries to each other giving an inflection to their voices which make it sound as though they were discussing something in a living room rather than simply making a noise. On rare occasions we have seen eagles take small salmon from the water's surface. They can lift about a fifth of their own body weight and so are restricted to loads of two or three pounds. We have seen them take herring and lamprey from the water, but again this is rare. One day I watched as one swooped silently from the sky to pluck a small squirrel which had ventured onto a branch to sit in the sun. The manoeuver was very tricky because of the other branches about, but he picked that poor unsuspecting little squirrel off the end of that branch just as slick as a whistle.

Photographing your salmon as they jump while you are playing them is difficult but fun. Be sure to take some shots of the fish you catch and the people who caught them because in the years to come they will bring back fond memories.

As you approach the area you are going to fish, watch for feed. You have to watch the surface of the water just as carefully as you would look at a road map. The feed may be otherwise marked, perhaps by gulls or by diving birds. Make a circle of the area before you begin your fishing, checking the areas along the shore. Look beneath the surface of the water right down into the depths from time to time.

If you spot feed then pull alongside. Try to determine the size of the herring, then try to match that size if you can with one from your herring bucket. Watch the surface for signs of finning salmon and below the surface for thrashing salmon, or herring scales, or Coho. Note the direction in which the herring are moving and note the current flow. If possible, avoid the use of an anchor and try just mooching alongside the school.

Let's assume that there are no herring for the moment, but you have spotted a flock of gulls pecking at the surface; you think it may be shrimp. Watch for the occasional little "v" on the water surface created by a shrimp swimming along the surface. The presence of these shrimp argue strongly for the presence of Coho in particular. The shrimp being near the surface, you can be sure the Coho will be found at a depth no greater than sixty feet. Coho are so enthusiastic in their feeding that they occasionally appear to be jumping but are actually misjudging the surface of the water in their feeding fury and coming right through it in what appears to be a jump. It may be that they are blinded by the densely-packed shrimp. Regardless, you will frequently see them appear to be jumping in the presence of this type of feed. Remember to strip your line out in the manner previously discussed; slowly and with pauses at twenty-five and sixty feet.

Never, ever strip line from your reel with the clicker or ratchet on. It is offensive to others, unnecessary, and marks you as an amateur. Keep your line from over-running by adjusting the center nut, putting on just enough drag to keep the spindle from revolving unnecessarily. Never have your tension too tight because you will be handicapped when you are called upon to reel in quickly.

In order to measure out your line accurately you have to know the distance from your reel to your first guide. On some mooching rods this is two feet, on some it is three. Assuming you are right handed, hold your rod in that hand across your body and strip the lines on the reel pulling it each time out from the reel to the first guide and counting, "two, four, six, etc." You must always know exactly how much line you have out so that you know at what depth you have had your mooch.

As you become more proficient you will notice your depth sounder showing, say, a hundred feet, but your count indicates you are hitting bottom at eighty feet. The reason for this is that your reel is over-running a little and you are playing out four feet instead of three; don't tighten your reel, simply change your count to "four, eight, twelve, etc." When the fish are deep, it's important to get that line down to them as quickly as possible. You may even find yourself counting by fives after a while.

If as you are stripping out in a hundred and fifty feet of water your line goes slack at forty feet you probably have a salmon with your herring in his mouth; you should put your ratchet on, change your rod from your right hand to your left and then reel furiously. Try to reel not with your arm or your forearm, but with your wrist, and your wrist alone, with a minimum of motion of the forearm. You can reel twice as fast using only your wrist as you can using your whole arm. You must also try to hold the rod nice and steady with that left hand because as you reel you should be watching your rod tip to see if it is bending to the fish.

If your rod doesn't bend over indicating the presence of a fish, then stop reeling and watch your rod tip. If it is completely slack, you know that your salmon is still there and still rising and you must quickly return to your reeling. If, however, the rod tip bends indicating that your weight and herring are there but not the salmon, then just leave it there for a few moments - give it perhaps a minute, and then slowly strip out six feet and wait a moment or two, then strip out another six feet. It may be that the salmon has risen with the bait and then decided to let it go but is still there and you can pick him up if you slowly drop the bait down to him again. You would be surprised how often this works.

If the rod bends over to the fish as you catch up with it, then you have to make your strike. Ted Peck, the broadcaster-sportsman, says that you have to hit that fish hard enough to break its back and he is right on. You have to really smack that fish. With your light rod, the natural stretch of the nylon, water resistance and the salmon's hard mouth, it takes a very healthy strike to set the hooks. You won't break your line no matter how hard you strike and remember that you want those hooks to sink in beyond the barbs. A salmon's jaw is mostly bone and it takes a real "whack" to set the hooks. Anything short of that will result in the salmon throwing the hooks when he jumps or they will pull out, generally towards the end of the fight when he turns sideways to you, presenting a new angle for the hooks.

Once you have struck him, let him go; the further the better, whether it be away from the boat or straight down. He will be easier to play if he heads away from the boat, so always encourage this. Keep your rod tip up at all times and by that I mean that the rod butt should be in your tummy and the rod should never be much more than six inches away from your nose. Never play a fish from the reel with your rod pointed at him like a gun. Keep your rod up so that the whole length of it bends with the fish; when he jumps, keep the tip up and back so that the line is always tight and the rod always bent. If he comes at you, reel quickly, again with the tip high.

Don't be in a hurry. Watch him in the water. Look for others coming around to see what is happening. Leave your other rod or rods at thirty feet, remembering that the more he flashes in and around the boat, the more likely you are to attract other salmon to the mooch. The object of the game is to tire him out and not to bring him into the boat in a big rush and net him as quickly as possible. You might even want to give him some slack line to see what he does. Note whether he faces into the current or whether he drops down; generally form some idea of the behavior of the fish. When he is really tired he will turn on his side. If you are alone, then wet your net and leave it handy. You should never put your net into the water until you are ready to take the fish into it. So many people lose fish because they shove the net into the water before the fish is ready to net and one of the hooks or both of them catches in the net and the fish simply breaks free.

Spring are particularly conscious of motion above the surface and you will find that the first time that the Spring actually sees you or the rod he will make a furious attempt to break loose and here you should simply let him make his run, bringing him back to the boat gently. Again, when you raise your net he will make another lunge for freedom and you may find that he makes several each time you bring him towards the boat. Coho do the same thing but they don't usually have the strength that a Spring has for these last minute rallies. Coho fight so furiously that I prefer to bring them into the boat a little quickly and net them with one quick swoop before they break into that last minute action which so often throws the hook. In the case of a Spring, however, you must take it really carefully.

Every now and again you will take a Coho that doesn't realize that he is hooked and comes up to the side of the boat as though there were nothing wrong. If you are on your toes, you can net him in one quick movement before he realizes what has happened. It is not something a novice should do, but happens fairly frequently during Coho season. It has often crossed my mind that there is something wrong with that particular fish's defence mechanism.

There has been, is now, and will in the future be just one way to net a salmon and that is head first. If you can't net him head first, then leave him alone. If you are netting a fish for somebody else, it is frequently wise to have him get away from the edge of the boat and back up to the other side of the boat to bring the fish in even closer. The actual netting motion should be one nice neat scoop into the water to take the salmon head first.

Your salmon net should be of linen twine so that it becomes wet quickly and hangs down. Do not buy the plastic type. Remember to wet the net before you make any attempt to net the fish or you will find that the net floats up and you are unable to get below the fish.

Once in the net the hooks will catch the mesh and he will be able to break loose, so lift the net with the handle at right angles to the water. This closes the net and also if it's a big fish you will break your handle if you lift it up like a pancake flipper. If you have a partner, by all means let him do the netting, keeping the fish "head up" for him and bringing it in head first; do not press him, or allow him, to net the salmon until it is thoroughly worn out. If he should lose the salmon, don't have a heart attack, he will feel badly enough about it without you chewing him out.

The Department of Fisheries operates a Head Recovery Program which is very important to the management of both sports and commercially-caught salmon. The program operates at two levels for the layman. The sports fishermen are asked to watch for marked salmon and then to remove the head from that salmon and deliver it to a Head Recovery depot where it will be picked up by the local Fisheries officer. The salmon are marked when they are small fry in the hatchery by clipping the little fin on the top of the body between the dorsal and the tail. This fin is called the vestigial or adipose fin. When this fin is missing the likelihood is that the salmon contains a coded tag which has been inserted in its nose when it was very small. Most marinas are head depots. The head of the fish is taken to the depot and a tag is filled out containing the date and the place where the fish was caught and some other informatin of importance to the Fisheries Department. They operate a raffle based on these tags with substantial prizes so there is a direct as well as an indirect advantage to the sportsman.

The Fisheries Department also operates a program which requires the sportsman to keep a monthly log. This log lists the number of times the fisherman has been fishing and the locations where he has been fishing, the number of people on the boat and the system of fishing used. A record is kept of the number of marked and unmarked Coho and Spring caught on each trip. By using these figures, the Fisheries Department can calculate how many tagged fish are among the total catch of any one sportsman. The reports are submitted by the fishermen monthly and by working backwards the Department of Fisheries can calculate roughly how many hours are spent in catching any one fish and can determine the ratio of tagged to untagged salmon caught by any one sportsman. It helps them to round out their statistical picture.

Cleaning and care of fish will be dealt with in another chapter, but for now you should know that any salmon under five pounds must be cleaned immediately. This is particularly so in warm weather. It is an easy matter to clean a salmon over the side of the boat and this will be explained later.

In the early months of the spring, depending upon the area where you are fishing, you will find that the Coho will probably not take a live mooched herring. Whether this is because they are immature or because they are, in the main, feeding upon shrimp spawn, I do not know. These small Coho are very attractive to catch because the flesh is fine and tasty. In addition, they thaw quickly, if you are freezing your fish, and so are easier to put on the table than a larger salmon. There are those that argue that these small Coho should be left alone and allowed to mature. At the present time there are no regulations against catching them but you will probably not be able to do so using mooching techniques. This will perhaps annoy you because you will be surrounded by fishermen trolling and catching them with considerable ease. The moocher must either forget about them or use trolling tackle. The tackle for these small Coho is light enough to enable the moocher to use his mooching rod. The tackle used is a small dodger and here you can use one of the pink plastic dodgers if you wish and a leader of about three feet in length and the lure should be pink or red. A small Tom Mack spoon which is red on one side is frequently effective. Three or four ounces of weight is adequate. The reason for the somewhat longer distance between the dodger and your lure is that these Coho are shy and they don't like to take a lure that is too close to the dodger. The distance between your slip weight and the dodger should be about six feet. You should put your lines out different distances behind the boat and here again, those distances vary between thirty and ninety feet. You should try and locate shrimp spawn in the water and wherever possible, troll at an angle to the current, varying the speed of the boat and turning frequently. Making the boat travel in little crescents is frequently productive. We generally resort to trolling for these Coho on one or two mornings of the year because we like to have a few for the table.

It is a mistake to hold your rod while mooching because it makes it impossible to read the action of the tip. The rod should at all times be in a rod holder. There is no exception to this rule save of course that you must take the rod in hand when you are about to reel up and strike the fish. At all other times the rod should be in a rod holder and the rod holder should be of such a design as to enable you to remove the rod swiftly and easily from the holder in preparation for the reeling in and the strike. We use the simple wire rod holders held onto the side of the boat by blue plastic holders. I make a few little changes in their shape to enable the rod to be removed more easily.

There are two or three separate and distinct types of mooches which you must learn to identify and know how to handle. A large part of the mooching art is knowing when to reel in and strike that fish.

With Coho you are going to have a series of little tugs on your bait causing your rod tip to bend slightly each time. The general rule here is to let him take the bait. Simply remove your rod from the holder, watch the tip and stand prepared to reel. When your tip goes down and stays down, then reel in until the rod is arched and then strike him. Seldom will your Coho take the herring and rise with it causing your line to go slack. This is more the Spring type of take. If it ever does go slack you must of course reel just as quickly as possible and strike.

The Chinook mooch is something else again. Bear in mind his feeding habits and remember that you must watch that tip at all times and watch it intently. There is no sense in turning your back to it or chatting idly without looking at it. Sometimes it will move less than an eighth of an inch to signal the presence of a Spring. The rule here is to calmly but quickly lift the rod from its holder, disturbing the tip as little as possible; if the tip is still depressed, even by as little as an eighth of an inch, but definitely depressed then treat it as a strike, reeling in as quickly as you are able in the expectation of the rod arching down to the salmon. There is no firm rule as to how far to reel in one session of reeling. This comes with time, instinct and practice. I generally reel in at least forty turns of the reel before pausing briefly to see if he appears to be still there. It is important to try to keep the rod tip as still as possible while reeling because it can tell you if you are still in contact with the fish which may still be rising so quickly that you can't actually strike him. The rod will naturally have some bend to it just because you're reeling your herring in quickly and the trick here is to be able to tell when the bend is such that you are reasonably sure the salmon is still there. If you pause in your reeling and the rod tip is perfectly normal, that is to say, it has its usual bend but no sign of any fish, just wait a few moments and then strip off six feet of line and wait again, then six more feet. What you are trying to do is to drop the bait back down to him. If you pause in your reeling and the rod tip indicates no weight at all, then it is telling you that the salmon is still rising with the bait and you must return to your reeling. You have to time your reeling exactly but this will come with practice. Some moochers just leave the rod in the holder until the Chinook either swallows the bait, hooking himself, or leaves. This is not a good system because he will only oblige you about one time in ten. The art is to hook him while he has the herring in his mouth and this is the reason for the second hook and for using number six hooks instead of number tens. Only care, experience and concentration will lift you above the average for this technique. Some people have it almost naturally, others never excel.

Sometimes the salmon will let go of the bait just as you stop reeling and you will see that he no longer has hold of it but the problem will be that he has continued to rise a little and he is above your bait looking for it. I sometimes, instead of paying out six feet of line and then another six feet, reel it up ten feet to bring it up into his line of vision again. I do this and wait a moment or two, then gradually lower it. Naturally if he is above the bait there is no way that he can see it. Remember that if your rod tip indicates that the salmon has simply hit the herring a sharp rap, it sometimes helps to play out from three to ten feet as though he had stunned your herring.

There are some days when a person just can't do anything right. I recall one day off Thormanby Island when I had missed mooch after mooch. It seemed as though I was striking them too quickly. I resolved to be really patient with the next fish when it took. They were mostly Coho but for some reason just were not taking the bait well. Finally my rod tip gave that little bend but I didn't move save to take the rod gently from the rod holder and stand ready to strike. The salmon moved off away from the boat and rose from a depth of sixty feet where he had taken the bait up towards the surface. I knew that I stood a fairly good chance of setting the hooks if I could strike it while it was moving away from me and once its course of travel seemed clear, I decided to make my move. I really hammered it a good one but the Coho must have turned just in the second before I struck because the hooks pulled free. I reeled in my line to look at my herring and was quite surprised to find that side by side with my herring was another herring of about the same size but without any skin on it. My hooks had actually been swallowed by the Coho so that when I struck him I had pulled from his stomach a herring that he had eaten some time before. This shows to some extent the necessity of fishing with razor-sharp hooks. Not one of my six hook points caught that fish even though he had swallowed my herring right down into his stomach. Incidentally, he had taken my herring down tail first while the herring I took out of his stomach had been swallowed down head first so that they lay side by side head to tail when I brought them into my boat.

A Chinook may play with your herring for several minutes before finally taking it in his mouth for long enough to enable you to strike him. You will see your rod tip depressed, then relax, then depress again such that very often you will be tempted to give it a try, hoping to strike him on one of the short duration dips in your rod tip. You should resist the temptation. Wait until the tip depresses, no matter how little, but *stays* depressed; that's the time to really work on that reel until you are well into him and then strike him.

Let us suppose that you have fished the area of the euphausid shrimp using the techniques discussed in this chapter and taken nothing. There may be no easy answer to the problem; no matter how well you fish, you are not going to hook anything if they are not there. It could be that there is so much shrimp spawn at hand that your bait just doesn't stand a chance. If you have seen salmon surfacing or jumping, then you know of course that they are there and you should continue in your efforts.

It is reasonably common knowledge that when fish are jumping they are down about thirty-five feet below the surface of the water. They rise up through the shrimp or the herring and sometimes shoot right out of the water in their efforts to catch the feed. The one exception to this is that beginning in September spawning salmon jump as part of their river-ascending process. These jumping salmon may be any one of the five species of Pacific salmon that frequent our coast - Spring, Coho, Chum, Sockeye or Pink. This latter type of jumping salmon can be very frustrating and I always feel a little sorry for people when they circle around and around an area where these soon-to-be-spawning salmon are jumping because they very, very seldom take a lure. The only exception to this of course is that the little Pink salmon will sometimes take a "hot-rod" lure if it is cast in front of them and maneuvered in a certain way as they lie at the river mouths waiting to ascend the stream. You see people fishing for them in this manner quite often at the mouth of Indian

River in Burrard Inlet. This type of fishing has never appealed to me — somehow it seems a waste of time to catch a nearly-spent salmon in a river mouth when there is so much other fishing available.

Assuming that everything has failed in your efforts to secure a salmon at or near some shrimp spawn you should give it up after about half an hour or so. Let's assume now that you want to try a little shoal that you can see on a chart or of which you have knowledge. You will have to calculate which way the current is flowing - look right down into that water and try and see which way the plankton are drifting and then using your depth sounder, find the lee side drop-off of the shoal. That is to say, the side which will protect the herring from the moving current. Remember that the water has to speed up considerably in its effort to get up, over and around the shoal. Calculate which way you will drift, remembering that the wind may be working to your disadvantage. It may be blowing you into the current instead of allowing you to drift with it. This is an annoying situation and may require that you anchor. The trick is to try to make your drift with the tide so that your bait appears to be carried along by it. Position your boat so that you will drift over the drop-off and then lower your lines putting one at forty-five feet, one at sixty and one just off the bottom. After you have drifted over the drop-off and out into the deep water, start up your boat and bring yourself back over the shoal to repeat the drift.

If you have decided to anchor for one reason or another, you will find that the swiftly-moving water on the shoal may cause you considerable difficulty. If your boat is going to be swept along by the current rather than borne by the wind, then go well up onto the shoal and lay your anchor and then pay out line until you are right over the drop-off. If, on the other hand, you have to anchor in the deep water because the wind is moving the boat rather than the current, you will have much more difficulty. Sometimes you will find that you have had to let out so much anchor line that your boat is whipping back and forth so that one moment you are fishing in thirty feet of water and the next you are fishing in three hundred. There is nothing particularly wrong with this unless the action is so sharp that it leaves your lines on the surface all the time. If you want to stabilize the boat in one particular spot, then take the anchor rope from its cleat on the bow of your boat and tie it to a cleat on the port or starboard side. This will have the effect of causing your boat to swing in the direction opposite the side you have secured the anchor line and you will stay in one spot.

Once anchored you can try a variety of different depths for your lines, remembering that the herring will be below the level of the top of the shoal and so will the salmon. You can try one line just even with the top of the shoal and the other two down to the bottom which in this case will really be the steep side slope of the shoal. The salmon like to cruise along the lip of the shoal, sometimes even with it, but often about thirty feet below the actual lip or edge of the shoal, enabling them to nab anything that is swept off the shoal as well as to feed on herring schools lying in the lee of the shoal.

Such drop-offs are excellent for fishing lingcod which use the same technique as the salmon use. Lingcod simply swallow the bait tail first and keep right on moving which causes your rod tip to bend in a steady arc and finally draws line out from the reel. I landed a forty-two pounder one day after a half-hour struggle; the stomach was strangely distended so when I filetted her I took a moment to open the stomach which I do not normally do with lingcod and was surprised to find a five-and-a-half pound Pacific cod, still fresh, which had been swallowed tail first without so much as a toothmark on it. The Pacific cod was so long that the tail was curved around half the length of its body. It's a rough life down there on the ocean bottom.

These big ling, that is to say, over twenty pounds, are all females so we usually just shake them loose unless they are particularly numerous in an area in which case we will take a few. They fillet rather poorly compared to the smaller males and the meat tends to be considerably coarser. In any ling you may notice the odd dark mark in the flesh as though someone had driven a toothpick in and broken it off. These are rockcod spines that have broken off in the ling, and they are easily cut out with the point of a knife.

Sometimes, as with dogfish, both or even all three baits will be taken by a big ling with the result that all three rods must be used in playing the same fish. Do not use the net to bring a ling into the boat. It is much more easily handled by gaffing it in the head — under the jaw or through the gills. It should then be lifted clear of the water and dispatched by hitting it right over the eyes with a club. Don't bring it into the boat until it is dead because they really thrash around when they hit the floor.

If you happen to hook a little ling and want to release it, it is quite easily picked up by inserting two or three of your fingers in the gill cover as it is lifted just clear of the water. Once you have hold of the gill cover the ling, for some reason, will not move. He will just hang there patiently while you work the hooks loose and he won't so much as flap a tail. You won't want to do this with the big ling so when you have ascertained that it is a big female simply cut your leader off as close to her jaws as you can. The hooks won't bother her in the slightest and will rapidly deteriorate.

If the drop-off on the shoal doesn't produce keep your eye open for gulls feeding on the shoal or alongside it. Sometimes there are pockets or hooks along the edge of the shoal which harbor herring and these can often be very productive. If you spot gulls feeding on the reef, then pull up your anchor immediately to investigate, applying the same techniques you used with the euphausid shrimp. If all this fails, then try troll-mooching on the reef itself and back and forth along the drop-off of the reef, remembering to stop every now and again on the reef or its edge to let the lines settle.

There is a spot on the east side of Texada Island which holds one hundred and forty feet of water for a distance of about sixty yards. The bottom to the south rises quickly, having only sixty feet of water for quite a distance, while the bottom to the north drops off deep and fast as does the bottom if you move further out from shore. This spot nearly always holds fish no matter which way the tide is running. I suspect that when the tide is running to the south it is a traveling route for fish northbound.

There are certain spots that nearly always produce salmon. These spots are often very small in area. There is one at the south end of Texada Island; there are others at Bertha Rock off Thormanby and at Salmon Rock near Gibsons. Some of these areas can be readily understood because of their configuration but others I suspect are simply areas that are on a travel route for the salmon. These spots, if near a settlement, are generally marked by one or two moochers in car-top boats, a rod over each side quietly plying their oars. Often a charterboat will mark the spot, having arrived early to anchor in the most favorable lie. Here again, you should drift by him if at all possible. If you do have to anchor, be sure to give him lots of room.

Very seldom do I fish as late as twelve noon, having started somewhere around six in the morning. Usually we come in and clean the fish, take a shower and sack out for a few hours if we want to tackle the evening mooch. When the Coho are running, we often stop short of our limit by one fish each if we plan on the evening mooch in the hope that we will hit a big Spring just before dark.

As the evening moves in, say from 4:00 p.m. on, you will probably want to fish a bay or some area where the land mass will give protection to the feed and to the salmon for the night. Calculate your tide, then pick your spot. Feed becomes very important at this time of day so keep a sharp eye out for the signs of it. The salmon will enter the bay in one of two ways; either they will enter the bay at its deepest point right down the center of the bay or they will sneak around the corner, following the shoreline in the deepest depth that they can attain while keeping about fifty feet from the shore. They will be looking for feed so that they will break right or left after entering the bay to search along the shore. Frequently they will settle just inside the bay corners where the feed will first enter if the tide is filling up the bay. Only experience in any particular bay can teach you the best spots. Different bays have different bottom configurations which affect the flow of the current.

This evening mooch in the bays or their entrances has been for me the epitome of all that is beautiful about mooching. The pleasure of the setting sun; the shimmering iridescent water; the ever-changing colors of the sky and clouds; all combine to form a scene of beauty painted as only God can paint. This always seems to be such a quiet time of day; the silence broken only occasionally by the call of a seagull or loon. To share this with a companion comes as close to heaven on earth as man can ever come. In these rare moments I have had both the time and the inspiration to review my past and plan my future. It is a time of reflections, both inside and out, with those outside brightening those inside. It is truly a time to talk with one's self and one's God. For me it often brings a sense of humility and of perspective. Any salmon caught is just a bonus.

12

The Fish You Will Catch And How To Handle Them

It will be some time before you will be able to tell what you have on your line just by the feel of the rod, but with experience this will come to you. Each fish has its own distinctive way of fighting, although of course you are frequently fooled. Part of the mystery of mooching comes with trying to figure out exactly what it is you have on your line before you bring it to the surface. From time to time you will hook something that you cannot bring to the surface. It will simply take your line and move off a few feet and stop and then move off a few more feet and stop. My guess is that these are skates which are common along the British Columbia coast at moderate depths. I saw one washed ashore at English Bay once that was six feet long and must have weighed close to two hundred pounds. There is no way that you can raise these on your fifteen-pound test line so the only thing to do is break it off.

I can never talk about big fish without recalling an incident recounted to me by a fellow who lived on a floathouse up in Thompson Sound at the mouth of the Kakwieken River. I had traveled up there to try a little fishing in the river mouth and this fellow let me tie up at his float. He told me that one time he had lowered his crab trap off the float as was his habit when he was surprised to find that the line had suddenly gone slack. The net was of the double hoop type with the open top rather than the box-trap type and he saw it suddenly appear on the water surface about sixty feet away wrapped around the head of a huge halibut which had seized one of the salmon heads in his mouth. The halibut was brought up short when the quarter-inch line suddenly went taught from the net to the spike on the dock where it was secured but the halibut snapped that as though it were a piece of cotton. The fellow was upset at losing his crab trap because such things are hard to come by in those areas but he had to admit it was quite a sight.

The correct handling of fish at boatside will enable you to return most of the fish you don't want to keep without harming them. Salt-water fish are hardy creatures although there is presently a solid conflict of opinion as to the survival rate of salmon brought to boatside and then released for whatever reason. Tests carried out by the Fisheries people argue strongly for the proposition that the casualty rate is high for salmon caught and then released. They say that the fatigue toxins built up in the salmon's system frequently bring about its death. Sportsmen say the tests were poorly done because the salmon were not returned to the sea, but instead kept in a holding tank for observation. The tanks being a poor substitute for a natural environment, the casualty rate was high. Unfortunately, I did not read about the results myself and I have a suspicion that the salmon were caught with commercial gear and, of course, that one fact alone would make the tests meaningless. One can well see that a salmon caught on a lure behind a twenty-five pound ball and then brought to the surface is going to be in vastly different shape than one that is brought to the side of the boat on light mooching tackle.

I have often caught "kelts" while river fishing; these are steelhead that have spawned but which may live to spawn a second time. They take a lure readily, being voracious feeders, and are easily identified by their coloration. I always release these fish because I feel that they are such a rare trout. I have yet to see one die on me — the fish usually swims away quite cheerfully to resume its lie in the river and can be seen in the same spot hours later, holding its own against the current and seemingly in good health. One day I actually hooked the same stupid kelt twice, much to my annoyance. It seemed to be doing fine even after I had released it the second time.

My experience with the kelt taking twice in the same day is not at all an unusual experience; frequently fish just released will take a lure a short time later. The number of salmon that we have caught bearing really terrible scars would indicate that they are much hardier than the Fisheries' test indicate. Certainly a wound elsewhere than in the gills does not usually cause death. Any damage to a salmon's gills usually results in it bleeding to death almost immediately. The removal of a large number of scales in the handling of a small salmon is fatal to the fish.

The issue is important because when the fishing is really hot, moochers frequently release the smaller Springs, even six and seven-pound fish, in the expectation of catching a really big one, particularly if they have already boated two or three salmon. The law is clear that you can continue to fish and release your fish providing you have caught and killed fewer than your limit on any given day. The practice is frowned upon by the Fisheries Department because of the fatigue theory. Some moochers have a different system; if they have two or three in the boat and hook a small one, they will row over to another boat — usually a tourist — giving the fish slack line and offer their rod to someone who wants to fish - generally a youngster aboard. It's a nice thing to do and leaves the moocher with the promise of a bigger fish and a chance to continue fishing and yet provides a salmon to a boat that might not otherwise have one.

If you are going to release the salmon, you should bring it to the boat as quickly as possible. Leave the fish in the water, perhaps holding it against the side of the boat with the leader, and use your pliers or your hook remover to extract the hook. If the hook is outside the fish where you can see it, this is an easy procedure. With patience you can remove hooks almost anywhere in the mouth. A hook in its throat is very difficult. Don't worry about a mouth wound or bleeding from the mouth — the salmon will quickly recover from this. If you can't get at the hook then quickly net the fish, bring it aboard, leaving it in the net, and go to work on it. Then just drop it overboard from the net or scoop it over by putting your wet hands under its belly. If the fish you are trying to release is under the legal size limit, you must release it regardless of how badly you damage it because you cannot keep an illegal fish for any reason whatsoever. If necessary, return it to the sea dead.

To kill a salmon that you are going to keep you should hit it forward of the eyes with your fish club. To strike the salmon back of the eyes or at the back of the head will cause the flesh to be bloodshot. The force of the club explodes the blood into the flesh so that when you come to clean the fish you will have an area extending two or even three inches into the nice flesh of the salmon which is all discolored. To pound the fish head with repeated blows landing all over the head area is most definitely not the way to do it. It is considered to be in very poor taste to gaff a salmon and you should always use a net. Aside from the fact that it avoids damage to the flesh, it is both easier and safer.

No doubt you will catch many rockfish. There are over forty different species and you will learn to recognize them or at least a few of them. I have given up trying to remember all the different names because as fast as I learn one, I forget another. There are other bottom fish such as the thornyheads and a variety of sculpins. The sculpins definitely aren't worth keeping, but most of the rockfish can be filetted or cleaned for the table. The meat is delicious, being completely white, very light, and flaky. Although they are highly edible, they certainly present a problem to clean. There are no catch limits on rockfish. When they are at boat-side you should lift the head clear of the water then reach down and grasp the lower jaw with thumb and forefinger. There are no teeth to worry about, but watch the spines along the dorsal fins —they are very painful because they contain a mild poison. If you can't get the lower jaw open, then you can generally pick it up safely enough by the sides of the head. Many is the time when I have been trying to get that lower jaw open to get at the hooks when I have allowed the spines to catch in my tummy. It certainly wakes you up. We don't bother to keep the rockfish so we remove the hooks while they are alive and I have both needle nose pliers and an ordinary hook remover to assist if I can't get them out with my fingers. If you intend to keep the rockfish give it a whack just forward of the eyes before you remove the hooks. If you plan to return it to the water you will be pleasantly surprised to see that it nearly always survives. Sometimes it needs a little push with a rod tip to wake it up but it will then dart down to the bottom.

The most beautiful of the rockfish is the yelloweye rockfish which is known everywhere as the "red snapper." They grow to about three feet in length and are brilliantly red when first caught but the color sometimes fades after death. To be exact, it generally loses its color at death but the color later returns. They are much bigger than most other rockfish but unfortunately they cannot stand pressure changes. When you bring them up to the surface they frequently have a large air-filled balloon protruding from their mouth. I generally keep them because they won't survive in this condition but have experimented with a system of puncturing the air sack with my knife tip and the prodding the sack back into the fish's throat with the spoon end of the knife. It only takes a moment and when dropped overboard the snapper quickly returns to the depths. Whether they survive or not I don't know, but I am willing to bet that they do.

Every now and then you will catch a bocaccio which is known in these parts as a "sea bass." They give you a real good scrap for the first few minutes and are a real sports fish. They have a large mouth with a lower jaw protruding well past the upper jaw. They grow to three feet in length, but these big ones are deep. Again, you can pick them up by the lower jaw for hook removal, but they are a vigorous fish and therefore a firm grip is required. They are delicious eating and not too difficult to clean. Where you catch one, there are sure to be more. Bocaccio, of course, means "big mouth." They are a deep brown in color and this color is fairly uniform the length of the fish. Some years you can't keep these bass off your line, other years go by without our catching even one. We find this to be true of many species of fish.

Among the prettier fish you will encounter are the various greenlings. There are five different kinds; the rock greenling, the kelp greenling, the white spotted and the little masked greenling and the painted greenling. The latter two never exceed a foot in length. They are hard to tell apart, but all have tiny little mouths with thick, distinct lips.

Most people call these fish "tommy-cod" but this is a misnomer. A tom-cod has a tiny barbel, which is a fleshy whisker, under the chin and they never exceed a foot in length. Some of the greenlings will reach nearly two feet.

The mouth of the greenling is too small to permit you to pick it up by the lower jaw so, as with the lingcod, if you intend to release them you must grasp them by inserting your fingers behind the gill plate from the belly side and hold them by that. It sounds like a strange way to hold a fish, but it's easy to do and again, fish held this way seem to quieten down just like a cat will when picked up by the scruff of the neck.

Greenling are fine eating, but they are so pretty and there is so little meat on them that I seldom keep them.

Every now and again you will encounter hake. The correct name for them is Pacific hake but all the locals call them "herring hake." If they show up in any number you will have to quit mooching or else resort to power mooching because they will go through a dozen of your herring in no time flat.

The first time we encountered one I tried to pick it up by the lower jaw. The teeth are quite sharp but by arching my thumb a little I succeeded in holding on to him. He promptly closed his mouth firmly on my thumb, the only fish which has that ability. My partner nearly fell overboard laughing. I didn't think it was very funny at the time, but perhaps that's because I was looking for a pair of pliers to force his mouth open. The teeth only scratched me but the surprise of it scared me. We have since learned that they generally swallow the hooks so completely that removal is impossible. Now we just take a quick swipe at them with a knife, cutting them in half as they hang from the line and then cut the leader. They are not commonly eaten, the flesh being very soft and fishy tasting.

A fine eating cod is the Pacific cod. These beautiful fish are recognizable because of their large mouth and a barbel under their chin. They are much bigger than the tom-cod, have white bellies and are fairly uniformly brown with little swirls. These must be picked up by the gill plate which you can do quite easily while they are still in the water. They are called "black cod" by the locals but the true black cod is the sablefish which looks much like a Pacific cod but has no barbel and only two dorsal fins and one anal fin. The Pacific cod has three distinct dorsals and two distinct anal fins. The sablefish smokes beautifully and is used commercially to make the famous "Alaska black cod." Both the Pacific cod and the sablefish are very important commercial fish.

If you are confused at the variety of fish described here, don't be. It will all clear up to you after an hour or so spent in your local aquarium. It is fun to be able to recognize your fish and important to be able to name them correctly. You will almost never catch a sablefish in Georgia Strait — I don't know why but there just don't seem to be many about. Pacific cod are reasonably abundant here.

The best of the cods and the most sought after is the lingcod. These are truly a magnificent cod, easy to fillet and great on the table whether as fish and chips or fried or steamed. They freeze well and when cooked, the flesh is absolutely white and very light and flaky. Many people prefer it to salmon. The males seldom weigh more than twenty pounds but the female can attain a length of five feet and can weigh a hundred pounds. Forty and sixty-pound females are quite common. These fish are found at any depth but unlike most bottom fish will rise a considerable distance from the bottom to take a lure. They are fast enough to hit a trolled lure and when we are fishing for them we quite often troll-mooch, allowing our live herring to settle slowly towards the bottom but then moving the boat before it gets down much lower than forty feet in order to avoid the rockcod.

The landing of a really big one takes time and patience for she will rise a short distance then make a rush back to the bottom and you have to start all over again. When we learned, compliments of the Fisheries Bulletin, that she lays nearly half a million eggs — nearly thirty pounds of them — we started to release these big females. Experience will tell you when you have one on and it is a simple matter to give the line a jerk which either snaps the fifteen-pound test leader or pulls the hooks loose. The hooks are no impediment to her at all because she has such a huge mouth. The gullet also is huge and the salt water rots out the hooks in a short time.

Some ling show a beautiful green and others a beautiful blue color throughout their own natural coloration. This color is in the flesh, too, giving it an eerie appearance. The color disappears on cooking and does not affect the taste at all. I understand that the coloring is caused by their diet.

Old timers know that lingcod eat rockcod and they will often kill a small rockcod or use a live one as bait to catch a big ling. This trick works only if there is a big enough ling around to take the bait. In certain areas we fish, when we hook rockcod, a big ling will nearly always grab the rockcod and hold onto it for a while, letting go only when it gets near the surface. You can feel the weight of it come on and stay with you, then let go, and when you bring your rockcod in you will find the ling's teethmarks on its sides. A ling will frequently disgorge itself just as it reaches the surface. As explained before, if you are going to release it, you simply pick it up by inserting your fingers under the gill plate near the belly and lift it free of the water while you remove the hooks. Never, ever grasp it by the lower jaw because it has a set of canine teeth that are really impressive and which can inflict a fair wound. I'm quite sure that lingcod attack each other because they frequently bear scars which could only have come from another set of lingcod teeth. They are a truly beautiful fish and highly valued. As explained in an earlier chapter, gaff them below the lower jaw, lift them clear of the water and club them while they are still outside the boat.

An unusual little visitor to your bait is the squid. They travel in schools and are generally forty feet below the surface. You will feel a little tug at your herring, but when you strike it, there is generally nothing there; when you check your herring you will find it has a little piece of flesh nipped neatly out of his back just behind the head, almost square in shape. The squid has a beak just like a parrot's beak with which he neatly kills the herring before dining. If you happen to hook the squid you will find that it puts up a pretty fair fuss when it reaches the surface, squirting water all over the place in its attempts to free itself. It is seldom hooked very firmly so when you have one at the surface a little jerk on your line will generally free it. One evening I decided to net one for the children to take to school. It came into the net nicely enough but broke free of the hooks just as the net encircled it and as I swung the net overboard it slipped through the net onto the floor of the boat. It was about a foot long and when I picked it up the little fellow grabbed me around the wrist with all its tentacles. Let me tell you I sure let out one hell of a yell as I flung it across the boat. I have never been so surprised by anything in my life. I am told that people jig for them here and there but we have never had one on board since. The only place I like to see them is on a plate with lots of mushrooms and tomato sauce. The Japanese relish them raw and I've eaten them that way; they are absolutely delicious. The flesh is smooth in texture and clean tasting. I have no idea at all whether or not they would try and take a nip out of you with that little beak, but I suspect that they would not.

You will frequently encounter dogfish while mooching. A dogfish, despite its appearance, cannot move quickly enough to take a trolled lure but does present a real problem for moochers. From time to time efforts have been made to interest people in eating them, but they just have not caught on as a table fish except in Europe. The flesh is firm, white and good tasting, but the appearance of the fish, which is a true shark, is just too much for most people to overcome. Besides, they are awkward to clean. These small sharks are not to be confused with "dog salmon" which is the local name for Chum salmon.

Dogfish are fascinating. The first thing to remember is that their teeth are razor sharp and you should avoid them. They are small but set in several rows, usually two but sometimes three and they can sever fifteen-pound test line very easily. We try always to bring them to the surface and kill them because they are a nuisance when fishing, both for the sports and the commercial fishermen.

At one time there was a commercial fishery for dogfish and they ranked third in importance behind salmon and cod. This was in the days when their livers were needed for the oil and the vitamin A content, but with the invention of synthetic vitamin A, the market collapsed. This was around 1950 and dogfish have been on the increase ever since. They are of particular trouble to the commercial fisherman; they destroy his gear and they attack salmon held in his nets. From time to time the government puts a bounty on them to reduce the stocks. Some commercial fishermen use the flesh as bait for prawn. We bring them to the surface, gaff them, then kill them with a knife. We never try to save the leaders because the dogfish skin is so abrasive that it frays them. The Haida Indians used to skin the dogfish and used the dried skin to sand their canoes.

One winter we were fishing a small bay with three other boats when we hooked a big dogfish. It came to the surface easily enough where I gaffed it. There were seven sets of hooks and leaders trailing from its mouth, all new and shiny. The other fellows were simply bringing it to the surface and cutting their leaders off below their weights. This is the only time we have actually seen solid evidence of the fact that a dogfish will stay around to attack the next bait sent down. I do not think that enough people realize how very scarce feed can be in the sea. Some winters when there are no herring about we find the salmon's stomachs containing an abundance of shiners. Once we gutted a Coho and then caught a dogfish ten minutes later with the entrails hanging from its mouth. There is no evidence, however, that cleaning a fish over the side of the boat attracts dogfish. They are either in an area or they are not.

Back in the days when I used to scale my salmon using a knife blade instead of a horse's currycomb, which I use now, I was scaling the last of a number of salmon over the edge of a dock just at evening time. The salmon started flipping about so I pulled it out of the water only to find a two-foot long dogfish firmly clamped onto the salmon's peduncle just above the tail. While the knife had been scaling away at one end, he had been chewing away on the other. He actually removed a little circle of flesh before I shook him off.

In some areas they are so profuse that when you bring one up to the surface you will see three or more swimming with him. Several times off Campbell River and once at Pender Harbour they have been so thick on the surface that the outboard bumped and chunked through and over them as they rasped against the bottom of the boat.

Dogfish give birth to their young live, generally eight or ten in number. They grow to a length of four or five feet and attain a weight of about twenty pounds. They live a long life for a fish, reputedly thirty to forty years. A lingcod lives about twenty years.

Dogfish have two dorsal fins and in mature fish there is a sharp spike protruding just forward of each fin. These are sharp so watch out for them if you are trying to grab hold of the dogfish tail. The best system that I have found is simply to bring the dogfish alongside the boat and gaff it. There is no easy way to kill it so the best you can do is to stab it with your knife blade in one or two places, then cut your leader and shake it off the gaff. These fish are so primitive that even cutting them in half does not kill them immediately.

Dogfish are predators. They destroy herring, prey on eulachon, eat crabs and generally are a nuisance. These facts are well known to the Department of Fisheries and this is the reason for the occasional bounty on them when they become too numerous. It will be some time before they become an acceptable table food, if ever, here in British Columbia. I am told that in England they are used regularly to make fish and chips.

From time to time you will bring to the surface a ratfish, recognizable by its grotesque head and snout with its little mouth and rat-like teeth followed by a long tapered body up to three feet in length. The gill slits are circular. They are fascinating in appearance and color. The males have claspers at the vent which can give you a bad cut. The eyes are a beautiful green. These fish were highly prized by the Indians along our coast for the oil their livers produced. It is extremely fine and durable and I have been told that it is still used to lubricate the moving parts of watches. They are so pretty that we make every effort to release them without touching them. Those front teeth are sharp and the claspers are dangerous. They feed on clams and crustaceans so they are probably capable of giving you a bad bite.

You will also encounter soles, flounders and turbot from time to time, all of which are very edible. You can either lift them aboard by the leader or pick them up as you would a hotcake. Only the turbot has sharp teeth and a mouth big enough for you to put a finger in.

There are very few fish that can harm you if handled with even a little care. Rockfish spines are painful but seldom infect; beware of the dogfish and the ratfish and handle your lingcod with care. Don't let me scare you away from squid — they are delicious.

One very important thing to remember is that when your rod is arched hard to a fish you are about to land, you must hold it in such a manner that if the hooks let go they will not strike you in the face. Never lean right over your leader because the force of a flying hook propelled by the suddenly-straightening rod will drive them deep into your flesh.

If you do drive a hook into your flesh past the barb you are in for a bit of a difficult time. There are a number of ways to handle the problem but by far the easiest is to go ashore and find a doctor and have him remove it under a local anesthetic. If there is no doctor at hand or if you feel brave enough, there is a system for removing them which the doctors actually use in the hospital. It takes a little courage but it works every time. The person doing it has to have confidence. You start off by making a loop of soft string — a shoelace does nicely. The loop can be made out of nylon but it is not as easy to work with as string. The loop should be about six inches in diameter. You slip the circle of string over your wrist as you would the loop of a dog leash and hold the rest of the loop in your hand such that you have a small loop at your fingertips to slip over the curved portion of the hook just as you would put a towing cable hook into the eye of a splice. You now depress the shank of the hook that is embedded in the flesh, pressing it gently against the skin. If the hook is embedded in a finger, the finger must be held absolutely solid, preferably by grasping it very firmly or pressing it against something and holding it down. You then snap the loop suddenly taut, snapping the hook out of the flesh through the same hole that it made going in. It takes a little confidence to give that loop a sudden jerk but that is what has to be done. It will not work if you tug at it or pull — it must be whipped out with a sudden jerk. It comes out so quickly and easily that the person in whose hand the hook is embedded seldom even knows that it has been removed. You must hold the finger firmly, however, otherwise it will simply jerk the finger loose and matters will be worse than ever. I have seen the doctors take hooks out in this manner on three or four occasions and I know that it works. Using this system they do not even employ a local anesthetic. Hooks in the strangest of places can be quickly removed in this manner. I would not want to do it were the hook anywhere near the person's eye, of course.

Another system, albeit a poor one, is to force the hook in an arc until it comes back out through the skin with the object of cutting off the shank and pulling it through and out. I have never done this because the embedded hook has never been placed in such a position as to make it feasible and when it has been feasible I have found it too difficult to force the point of the hook back out through the skin. Human skin is very tough.

13
Care and Cleaning

Most docks have a cleaning table with running water for the cleaning of your fish. The time you spend here can be fun if you take the trouble to share your experience with those who inquire. If you fish from the same dock with any regularity you will find among those inquiring people some of the finest friends you will ever make; fellow fishermen, old-timers, characters, dock bums, doctors, lawyers, actors, policemen — real down-to-earth men and women who feel at home in old clothes and sneakers. There are always children of all ages and dispositions.

If you have really been lucky there may be the odd snide remark, but even a snide remark has its humorous side. One memorable day we returned to the dock a scant three hours after we had left on a sparkling sunny July afternoon and were able to lay upon the dock in neat rows sixteen beautiful red Spring salmon from seven to twenty-two pounds, much to the chagrin of some of the local onlookers, for the Spring fishing had been slow. One of the fellows was late for something so he left his fish in our care. Of course everyone wanted to know where we had caught them, but we were reluctant to tell because we were worried that it might be a run which would be wiped out if a dozen boats suddenly descended upon the spot. We waffled and were vague as to the exact location and this must have miffed somebody because two separate people reported us to the local Fisheries officer which amused him highly because he had not only seen us catching them, but he had come aboard our boat for a sandwich. We hadn't wanted him to know how good the fishing was so we had casually left our herring down near the bottom. The Springs we were catching were sliding by at depths of forty-five feet to sixty feet, well above our herring, the water being one hundred and twenty feet deep where we were anchored. At the time that he had checked us we had eleven Spring on board, a fact he had carefully noted. Although we were friends, his job came first so he had had a pretty good look around, neglecting only to take the radio apart. The main thing was he knew there were four of us, not three. We waved him farewell, brought our lines up to sixty feet and promptly had the pleasure of seeing a rod tip genuflect.

That particular spot came to us as a result of the application of a combination of simple principles. It was an incoming tide so we rounded the island point to its lee; we found that there was an underwater shelf sloping out from the cliff then dropping off at sixty feet, abruptly, to a hundred and twenty. The fish were headed south into the tide but were using the island for protection from the tide flow, probably even stopping there momentarily. There was the odd herring plopping on the surface against the face of the cliff so we had had a lot going for us. In the days to come we would fish that spot only if things were really slow and then only when there was nobody about. It has a characteristic of being either red hot or absolutely barren. We estimate now that it is simply a spot past which the salmon swim in their slow migration down the coast. The photographs we have of those Springs sure bring back some fine memories.

The reason that that particular day comes to mind when I speak of fish care is that the system I am going to explain for cleaning and filetting salmon is based not so much on getting the last half ounce of flesh from the fish, as on getting most of the flesh from the fish in a reasonably quick manner. The proper cleaning of sixteen Spring takes a considerable amount of time so some of the systems that I have devised are designed primarily for speed.

Any fish weighing fewer than five pounds must be cleaned immediately for the flesh will soften and burn from the viscera acids. All Coho regardless of size must be cleaned as soon as they are caught for the same reason. Failure to clean Coho or small Springs will result in a deterioration of the belly walls of the salmon. When you have it cleaned you will see that the acids have actually attacked the flesh. Coho have a much softer flesh than do Spring salmon and for this reason require a very sharp knife if you are to avoid tearing the flesh.

The fish must be clubbed in front of the eyes as previously mentioned. The next step is to lean over the side of the boat and make a cut through the throat of the fish just below the pectorals cutting from the belly up toward the spine. The fish is held by inserting a finger into the gills on each side of the fish which is held such that the underside of its jaw is against the palm of your hand. The next step is to insert the knife blade down inside the belly opening through the cut that you have made under its throat and then make one nice long clean cut from the underbelly of the fish squarely between the two pelvic fins and ending just at the vent. The body cavity contents will start to fall and you can grasp the stomach and gently squeeze it to examine the contents. The cut that you have made through its throat will also have severed the esophagus. At this point you may want to save the roe from the salmon if she is a female and the "dry roe" if it is a male. This dry roe is one of the nicest taste treats imaginable. In a later chapter I tell you how to prepare it. I have not learned how to prepare the egg roe but I save this for a friend of mine who does some steelheading. I simply put both types of roe in one of a number of small plastic bags I have for this purpose.

Having set the roe to one side you can remove nearly all of the viscera with one smooth pulling motion. You should then run the tip of your knife blade down the membrane which holds the fish's kidney against the back of his body cavity just under the spine. The knife must then be reversed and the spoon used to scrape out the kidney. People often think that this is some sort of a blood groove that runs the length of the fish, but it is the fish's kidney and that is the reason that it has to be removed. It spoils quite quickly. Give this area a thorough scraping with the spoon on your knife and then wash out the body cavity thoroughly letting it trail in the water for several minutes if the boat is moving. All of this can be easily accomplished while you lean over the side of the boat. The fish should then be stored in a cooler or fish tank if you have one built into your boat. Water them down with a bucket of salt water every hour or so. It not only keeps them cool, but it also keeps the scales loose for easier scaling.

I use a simple horse's currycomb for cleaning the scales from the fish. It's very effective. You can buy one at most tack shops and in the Cariboo you can buy them in the fifteen-cent store. They only cost a couple of dollars so buy a spare.

Never put your just-caught fish in water to keep them fresh. They quickly become soggy. Never put them in a plastic bag, in fact any sack or bag other than burlap. Plastic seems to generate warmth and is always slimy, while most sacks or bags give the fish a curl which makes cleaning awkward. We find it best to lie the salmon neatly in a fish tank or a fish box or a large plastic cooler, occasionally pouring a bucket of salt water over them, providing the tank or box has a drain. A wet sack over your fish box is an excellent idea.

It always gives me pleasure to see Gordon Hill of the *Catto* slide into the dock. His boat is never cluttered, his rods are always neatly racked and his fish look as though he is going to have each one stuffed and mounted. He cleans them as he catches them. Contrast this to some fellow who dumps a curled slimy fish from a stinking plastic bag full of slime and blood. Yech. Salmon, if only for the aesthetics of it, should not be kept with your cod.

Assuming that you have a whole uncleaned salmon at hand, start by lying it on the cleaning table and giving it a quick splash of water. Then scale the fish from the tail up to the head using your currycomb or whatever device you have. Here it is handy to have somebody play water over the fish to wash away the scales as you work. Buying the occasional ice cream cone usually ensures a steady supply of small hands to carry out this interesting task.

Next you should wash all of the scales off the working surface. This should be done before you open the fish. Cut the tail off first as this helps to drain the blood from the tissues of the fish as you work on it. Next turn the salmon on its back; to remove both pelvic fins with one cut simply slide your blade under both fins and with the blade at right angles to the salmon, cut down briefly then along toward the head making the cut as shallow as you can.

Salmon have a little split in each pelvic fin so there is a sort of secondary little piece of pelvic fin you have to cut off and which you should watch for. Next, and with the salmon still on its back, you should remove the anal fin by making as shallow a cut as possible from the tail end toward the head of the fish. This cut should be made right through and past the anal opening to remove it also.

Now roll the fish onto its belly and remove the dorsal and adipose fin in exactly the same manner. Care should be taken in doing the dorsal fin for you will be again cutting toward your hand and the dorsal is often tough and spiny.

The next cut is simple; lie the fish flat with the belly toward you and with one cut at right angles to the board, remove the head and pectoral fins. Your blade will have to be slid under the pectorals but this one cut will remove the pectoral fins and the head.

If the fish is over fifteen pounds, you may wish to smoke it in which case you will want to leave the pectorals on and the casing of the body just where it joins the head. You must therefore make a cut that removes the head alone. You do this by cutting the appendage at the juncture of the belly and the gills then reversing the blade to cut off the head. I do not favor this system, choosing instead the other which is so much faster. If the fish is being smoked, the little holes made by the hanging hooks are nothing to worry about.

If you want to leave the head and tail on to show the fish or photograph it later, then you must remove the gills which are attached lightly enough at the various junctures inside the head. The gills tend to spoil quickly and so should be quickly removed. The removal is simple enough, just use the tip of your knife to cut around the gills where they are attached inside the head and pull them free.

Having made the one cut above explained, then insert the knife blade into the body cavity and cut the belly open all the way down to the vent. Pull the entrails out gently and squeeze the stomach from the anal end to force the contents out. They can tell you a great deal. Observe the contents carefully and try to visualize how they were injested. Note the size of the feed and try to match it when you buy your live herring the next time out. Check the pyloric caeca. The marked contrast between the Coho's few and the Spring's many will make itself apparent immediately.

Next you should wash the body cavity out thoroughly. Facing you but covered by a whitish membrane will be the fish's kidney held tight against the spine by the membrane and running the whole length of the fish. Make a cut down the membrane from the anal end to the head end and then use the spoon on your knife to scrape out every last bit of kidney, as I explained earlier. By pulling at the membrane you can remove that also. Now really give the cavity and indeed the whole fish a thorough washing.

It is now ready for cooking in whatever manner you please. If you like steaks, then you can cut it into steaks and wrap them in freezer paper or aluminum foil. We use foil. The wetter the fish when you wrap it, the better because freezing tends to draw the water out of whatever is frozen. In the commercial storage plants the fish are frozen whole by glazing them. The glazing is accomplished by spraying them as they freeze with a very fine spray to coat them with a thin layer of ice.

An excellent method of freezing steaks or cod fillets is to put them in a milk carton and then fill it with water before freezing. When we freeze our salmon, we wrap it while wet in aluminium foil, tight to the body or the flesh and this seems to work almost as well as glazing.

If you want to filet your salmon you should now place it on the table with the stomach open towards you and the tail end should be to your left if you are right handed. Your knife must be sharp. Place the blade on the spine where the spine emerges at the head end with the blade parallel to your cutting surface, cut the length of the fish in one long cut, working the blade along the spine with a slight back and forth cutting motion. Cut it right through down to the tail. You should be able to feel your knife blade riding along the spine as you make the cut. If you've done it right, there will be a little row of spots down the center of the filet where your blade has removed the covering from the spine itself.

You will probably ruin your first one because of a lack of confidence, but don't give up. The trick is well worth learning and well worth practicing. Having taken off that first filet, turn the fish over with the belly away from you and again if your are right handed the head end on your right. Place your blade on the spine at the head end of the fish and make a cut down to the tail in exactly the same way as you took off the first filet. The second filet is now free, leaving you with the spine which has almost no flesh on it. With practice you will learn to avoid the dorsal spines by lifting your blade a little as you pass them. If you have not done this, then you will have to cut the dorsal spines free with one simple little cut on one or other of the fillets.

If we are eating the salmon that day, I generally take the spine and cut it into pieces about two or three inches long. We call those "pork chops" and generally we fry them up in a little frying pan while we are waiting for the filets to cook elsewhere. They make dandy hors d'oeuvres.

The two filets you have will exhibit the chest wall rib bones running from the head end down to where the pelvic fins were. These are removed by a few minutes work with your knife tip. Start by slicing under them at the head end and working to the rear while pulling the loosened skin and ribs free with your fingertips.

There is still one row of very fine bones hidden in the flesh running from the head end down to about where the pelvic fins were. Most people leave them in but they can be removed if you wish. Some peole pull them out using pliers, but that is a lot of work. The best way to remove them, although it does take a very delicate touch, is to run your fingertips along the flesh from the head end toward the tail feeling the exact position of all the little bones. These bones curve slightly from the top where you can feel them down towards the belly just like the rib cage did before you cut the filets.

Carefully make a cut, allowing for the curve, from the flesh side down to the skin but not through the skin. You can actually feel your knife blade slide down the little row of bones. This cut will cause the flesh to part substantially and will look ugly, but don't let it scare you.

The second cut is the tricky one. You have to judge it just nicely and what you want to do is to make a "V" down to where the first cut met the skin. It's a little difficult and takes practice, but if you make that second cut just nicely you will meet the other cut just where it meets the skin. The bones will be embedded in the wedge of flesh thereby created. Now you gently pull, starting at the head end and using your knife tip to free it from the skin and remove the long wedge of flesh. At first glance it will look to you to be a disaster and you will wonder why you bothered with it and why you are taking such a big piece of flesh out of the fish. You will probably find that the flesh breaks a little or you may find that you have cut through the bones halfway down on your second cut. You will also find that as you get down to the tapered end of it that it is sort of hard to pull free and you will have to work your knife blade along the skin breaking it loose.

Then when it is done the filet itself will look ghastly with a big, long hole down the middle. Remember, however, that the flesh is opened up and that the wedge you took out is much smaller than it appears to be. Remember also that it is an absolute delight to serve somebody a filet that doesn't have even one little tiny bone in it. It is well worth the trouble and when the fish is cooked, it doesn't spoil the appearance a bit.

This particular bit of bone removal is harder to do in the Coho than it is in the Spring because the Coho flesh is so soft. It is also difficult to do in a small fish for the same reason. I might say that I'm the only person I have ever seen that makes this particular bone removal cut and it may not be appealing to you at all. I take a secret delight in serving people fish that doesn't have even one little bone in it. Older people particularly hate the bones and I don't mind making this cut. It takes a lot of practice and you will spoil the first few, but I think it is worthwhile sticking with it.

Next, wash the filets carefully making sure they are absolutely clean of any scales or pieces of wood from the cleaning board or chips of paint or whatever. We have experimented with a variety of ways of freezing the filets. To date the best system that I have come up with and one which really does seem to work very well is to use aluminum foil. I cut the filet into three if I want it in individual portions or I may just leave it whole, and then I let the water run on it, making sure it is good and wet. Then I wrap it in the silver foil just the way you would wrap a Christmas present, making sure that there is no way that any air can get into it. I generally accomplish this by lying the fish on the silver paper over it once, then folding the ends in and then continuing to roll it over

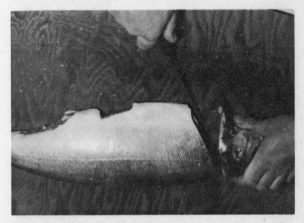

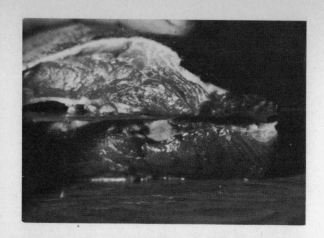

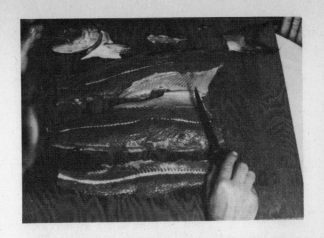

and over in the foil with the ends already in so that it is absolutely air tight. I make a point of not piling them in the freezer, but putting them in the freezer in such a way that the cold air can get all around them and they freeze very quickly. The fact that they freeze with all that water in the package makes them very moist when you do thaw them. The thawing itself in the silver paper packages is easily accomplished. You simply put the whole package in the sink and fill it with warm water. In ten minutes the filet is completely thawed and you can let the water run out of the sink and open the silver paper up and your fillet is ready to put in the pan. There are no scales to worry about, no bones, no mess. You simply rinse the sink out and cook the fish.

Using silver paper does have one drawback and that is that I haven't found a marking pen yet that writes on it very well. It is therefore sometimes difficult to label the packages. The solution that I have come up with is that I put a little fold in the corner of all the Coho packages just by folding the silver paper over a little and I know these are Coho. The Springs I leave completely flat. When I wrap my cod the bundles turn out round like a section out of a baseball bat instead of flat like a Christmas package so I know that they are cod. When I store the fish in the freezer, I always store it from left to right and remove it exactly the same way so that I'm not leaving any of it in the freezer for too long a period.

I suppose if you really wanted to take some care, you could have little gummed labels and put the species and the date it was caught and stick that to the silver paper.

Salmon wrapped in silver foil properly will, if it is a whole salmon, last for well over a year without any freezer burn or noticeable deterioration. I keep the freezer just as cold as the machine will go. At one time we used to freeze salmon whole but the thawing of a whole salmon is a lengthy operation and except for the largest family or when you are having in quite a number of guests the quantity of fish to thaw is really just too much. Filletting is far preferable and while it takes a little more work, it is well worth it. You should be able to do the whole operation from the scaling right through to the final wrapping of your filets in ten minutes for any salmon.

Something that should be mentioned here is that there are two distinct species of Chinook salmon - one is white and the other is red. The white Spring is not a red Spring which has been eating the wrong kind of food. The white Spring lays white eggs and has its own schooling habits and feeding habits. It runs into certain rivers - the Harrison River has a run of white Springs and I'm reasonably sure that the Fraser and the Squamish do also. These white Springs school together in the ocean and are comparatively rare. I am told by the Fisheries biologists that they are thought to have different feeding characteristics but they could not elaborate. A controversy exists as to which is the better table fish in the sense of which is the better tasting. There is no doubt at all that the red Spring has the better appearance and indeed many people don't like the look of the white Spring at all. It doesn't look like salmon because it's not red. When you open a can of salmon you expect to see a nice red flesh and that is what people expect when they are served salmon at the table.

I have several times take a portion of white Spring on one plate and a portion of red Spring on another plate, both cooked at the same time and in the same manner and then closed my eyes and had somebody feed me a portion of one and then a portion of the other and as a result of doing this test on a number of occasions, my taster tells me that the white Spring is the superior fish. It seems to be considerably moister and richer and somewhat smoother to the palate. I would be willing to bet that the oil content of the flesh is considerably higher than that of the red Spring. My Indian friends tell me that it is, and always has been, more highly prized by our coastal Indians because it smokes better and preserves better by smoking. This would indicate a higher oil content. If the fish that you catch isn't completely white, then it isn't a white Spring. Some red Springs are very slightly red or pink. I don't know the reason for this. I have a suspicion that these pink/white Spring, despite what the Fisheries biologists tell me, are fish that have been cross-fertilized. That is to say a white Spring has laid her eggs and a red male has fertilized them. Biologists I have talked to say this is impossible, but I think they may be wrong.

Arguments continue as to the style of fighting for each fish. Some fishermen maintain that the white Spring surfaces immediately and others maintain that the white Spring goes down and stays down. Some attribute the white with greater fighting qualities and other attribute the red. In twenty years of fishing, I haven't noticed any real difference. Some red Springs sound immediately and stay down and some red Springs fight all over the surface the moment you catch them. I think that a great deal depends upon the individual fish rather than the color of its flesh. Sometimes, too, the manner in which the fish is hooked will determine how it fights. A fish hooked in the lower jaw is generally a poor fighter because the moment he tries to run, he is putting the whole of his weight onto that lower jaw and he can't do this very well. A throat-hooked fish generally fights much better than one hooked in the jaw. A fish that will continually surprise you is a fish that is hooked in the side or the tail. He generally surfaces immediately and dashes away along the surface. He then stops while you pull him in backward. You will wonder what is wrong with him until you get him near the boat and see that he is side-hooked. Admittedly Coho are nearly always surface fighters but on occasion you will take a Coho down deep, really deep — say a hundred and forty feet, which is deep for a Coho and he will stay down there until he tires. A Spring hooked near a shallow ocean floor will generally run for deeper water.

We have a system of filletting lingcod which is really something to see. It is fast and very effective and very easy to do. The same system applies for any cod but the lingcod lends itself very well to this system. Filletting rockcod is always a difficult job because the rib bones are so thick and the system hereafter explained is not too effective for them, although it does work.

You lie the cod on the cleaning board with the back or dorsal fin surface towards you. If you are right handed, put the head to your left. You make one cut behind the head right down to, but not through, the spine. This is the first cut you make, without having gutted the cod or doing anything else such as scaling it.

Now insert your knife tip into the belly cavity through the cut you have made and make a cut through to just behind the vent.

Now insert your knife back into the first cut and turn the blade so that it is flat with the spine and parallel with the cleaning board. Holding the cod firmly by the head, you work your blade along the spine right down to the tail. At first your blade will be hidden by the wide filet but it will gradually emerge down near the vent. When your blade pulls free at the tail end you will be able to flop the filet over, almost boneless.

Now reverse the fish, putting the head to your right, repeat the process, but you will have to cut with your arms crossed as your left hand will be holding the head. You will now have two beautiful filets whether they be rockcod or a ling.

There will be a few chest-rib bones at one end of the filet and these are a little tricky to remove but you put your knife blade under the bones and slice up from the thin part toward the thick part pulling the bones free and then reversing the knife to cut down and free the ribs entirely.

The next step is really something to see. It was shown to me by Irene Burtnick from Sechelt. You lie the filet skin-side down and you make a little cut down near the tail end so you can hold it by inserting your thumb in the cut. You then take your knife blade and cut through the flesh to the skin but not through the skin. You turn the blade toward the head end of the filet and, holding your blade still, you pull off the skin by working it left and right as you pull the skin along the knife blade, holding the blade close to the board and parallel with it. The result will amaze you. The skin will come free, paper thin with absolutely no flesh adhering, leaving you with a perfect filet. No skin, no scales and almost no bones. It is all done very quickly and easily. You may ruin the first one or two but after that you will look like an expert. Incidentally, a salmon's skin can be removed in the same way.

The filet that you have at hand will be boneless except for the same row of bones that was in the salmon which are a secondary row of really small pin bones. They can be removed, but in a different manner than the salmon. Run your fingers down the flesh feeling for the little row of bones and do this a number of times until you know their exact position. Then slice the filet from the tail end right down through the head end, taking off the complete top half of the filet which does not have any bones in it but making that cut run just alongside the bones. You then make a cut along the edge of the bottom half of the filet removing the piece of flesh containing the bones. It doesn't matter that the cod filet ends up in two pieces because you will probably be doing that in the kitchen anyway. What you are doing here is simply cutting the bones right out of the filet. I then cut the two pieces left in half and have four nice pieces of absolutely boneless cod all ready for wrapping.

Rockcod and red snappers yield very little meat but can be filetted in exactly the same manner as the lingcod. After you have the filets off and the skin off the filets you can remove those chest-rib bones as previously described.

A distasteful subject that must be discussed here is the fact that from time to time you will encounter a tapeworm in your fish. These parasites have long flat bodies about a quarter of an inch wide and are yellowish in color and heavily segmented. That is to say, when you look at their bodies, you can see little flat lines across them much like the underside of a snake. These parasites exist in the intestinal tract of the fish only and never ever enter the flesh or meaty parts. Their larval stage requires a new and separate host; to do this the eggs are released through the fish's digestive tract but must find another victim in order to be able to develop. In the case of fish tapeworms, the new host is usually a small crustacean which is then in turn eaten by the trout or perch or salmon and only then does the larva develop into a tapeworm.

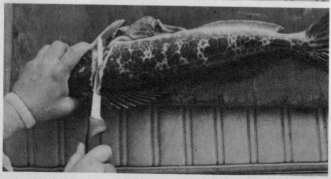

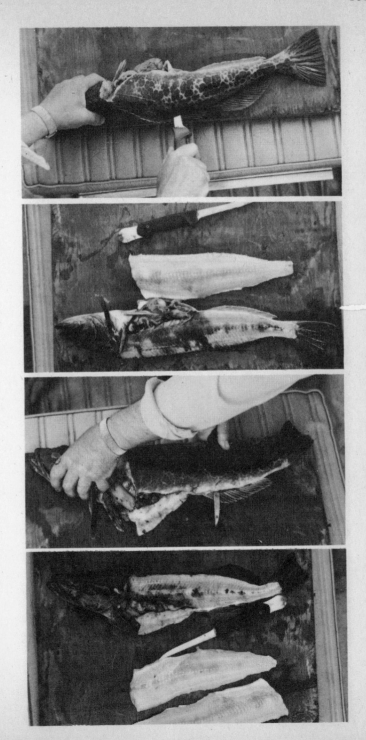

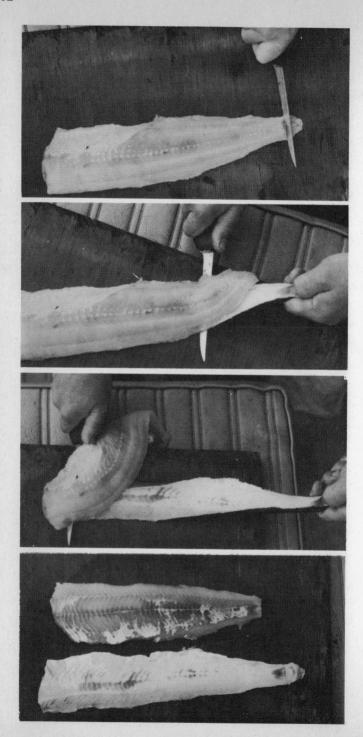

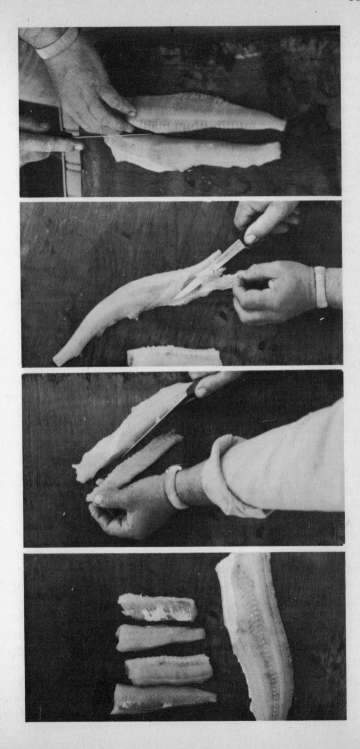

Man can of course become that host if the fish is not properly cooked. In some areas of the world almost all of the populace have tapeworms. Despite the fact that research into the subject indicates that tapeworms are not harmful to man, most people find it difficult to countenance the thought of one or more of these horrible-looking parasites dwelling within. If the fish is small or smallish then frequently I simply drop it overboard, clean the cutting board, and go on to the next fish. If it's a good big salmon and in good shape, I will often save it but am very careful to clean it thoroughly and to wash it thoroughly. I will never eat that particular salmon fresh, making sure that it is frozen, then thawed, before being eaten. The freezing of course kills any eggs and/or larva just as a thorough cooking does. The thought of any risk repulses one but the fact is that man is much more likely to incur these worms or their larva from pets such as dog and cat.

Occasionally you will encounter a salmon with dimpled skin and the scales disrupted here and there. It is almost as though it had a bad case of acne. These fish are frequently thin, being much too long for their girth. The disease is called furinculosis. This disease ruptures the tiny blood vessels and the fish gradually bleeds to death. The Capilano Hatchery has produced some Coho runs heavily infected with this disease in years past although the situation seems to be improving. It is of no harm to man and the fish is perfectly normal and can be eaten without danger.

It is always wise to cook your fish thoroughly, especially cod. The Japanese eat much of their fish raw in their sushi bars and sashami dishes but as they will quickly point out, all their fish used in these bars have been quick frozen and really frozen hard and then thawed and served. Vancouver has a number of these restaurants. The fish, when served "sushi" style, is laid on top of a ball of warm rice or rolled in a special dry green sea kelp with a touch of green mustard. It doesn't sound great, but it is one of the finest treats I have ever thrown a lip over. In "sashimi" style eating, the fish is served raw without rice but carefully laid out on a plate decorated with salad. The plate includes a little mound of green mustard. You pour a little soy sauce in the dish provided, add a little mustard and stir. You then dip each piece of fish in the soy-mustard mix and pop it in your mouth. The plate can include salmon, tuna, octopus, scallops, rockcod, halibut, herring, prawn, salmon roe, squid, sturgeon, gooeyduck clams, abalone, or mackerel, all absolutely raw. I have eaten all of them, many, many times and return again and again for this rare taste treat.

Each selection has its own particular flavor and consistency. From time to time I take a friend to the place where I enjoy the delicacies and never has the friend been disappointed. People who have never eaten a piece of raw fish in their life find themselves ordering second portions.

I have experimented with every way of cooking salmon that you could imagine. I have baked it in the oven and broiled it in the oven and barbequed it, poached it in water, steamed it, baked it in tinfoil and cooked it on sticks around an open fire. There is one system of cooking it that appeals to me more than any other. Since I now live alone, when I clean my fish I package them in one-meal portions wrapped tightly in silver foil. These thaw quickly in warm water.

I then take a teflon frying pan and put in about three tablespoons of nice light olive oil — Bertolli is a fine oil for this. I then take the fish and dry it using paper towelling and then I sprinkle it liberally on both sides with very coarse pepper. I then put the stove element on one reading lower than its hottest setting — that's a nine on my stove, ten being the hottest. I place the fish flesh side down in the oil and then I put a pot lid over the frying pan. The next step is a little hard to comprehend but I just let that fish cook in that very hot oil for about three minutes. You will experience a moment of panic when you see a cloud of steam and maybe a little smoke emerging from under the pot lid and you will think that you are ruining your fish, but the trick is to cook it fast over a very high heat. The cooking time varies according to the thickness of the filets and you will have to experiment with this. I then remove the frying pan from the element and, using a plastic spatula, I turn the filet over so that the skin side is down and I put it back on the stove and cover it again and leave it on that high heat for another three minutes. If your oil is susceptible to smoking, you can turn the element down as low as eight after a minute or so, but the hotter the heat, the nicer the fish. The trick is that fish which is overcooked seems to go dry so you have to judge how the fish is done by spreading the flesh with a fork and looking down into it. The moment it changes color from its deep red to pink, you have to take it off the stove and serve it. I have never tasted fish that appealed to me more than doing it this way and I strongly recommend it to you.

Fish generally needs some sort of a condiment or sauce to go with it but I am not much on sauces so I generally just have a little chutney — which goes very well with fish — or Worcestershire sauce or even ketchup if I'm desperate.

One day at Irvine's Landing in the Pender Harbour area, I

brought in a good size spring salmon filet and asked Maurice Green if he wouldn't mind cooking half of it for me and he could have the other half — I told him to charge me just the regular price for fish and chips and I would be happy to pay it. Naturally I expected him to fry it in the normal manner and serve it with a few chips but Maurice surprised me by cutting the salmon filet into finger-width portions, dipping them into his special fish and chip batter, then deep frying them. I had to admit that it sure is a great way to make fish and chips — using salmon instead of cod. You just won't believe how absolutely delicious it can be.

I couldn't wait to try it on my own so I bought a deep fryer and the oil and then more by good luck than good management I stumbled across a recipe for tempura batter in a cookbook that I have and started to use that. It is a very thin batter — it appears thick in the bowl, almost like porridge, but the fish doesn't pick up very much of it and then when you deep fry it you end up with your fish portions covered in a delicate thin brown crust — not the usual thick fish and chip batter that seems to soak up so much grease. This batter is really marvelous. If it has a drawback it is that you should let it sit for a couple of hours before you use it, but once made you can keep it in the fridge for days and it still retains its wonderful qualities. The recipe for it is as follows; you take two eggs and separate the yolks from the whites and then beat up the yolks. You then add a tablespoon of vegetable oil, a little pepper, one teaspoon of salt and one and one-third cups of ordinary flour or rice flour if you have it. You then add, stirring the while, three-quarters of a cup of flat beer. The batter has to end up fairly thick and the test for this is simple; you take a tablespoon of the batter and pour it off the spoon into the bowl. It should pour off the spoon for about an inch or an inch and a half before it breaks, leaving you with a little triangle of batter hanging from the spoon down about an inch or an inch and a quarter. When it is this consistency, stop adding the beer. You then cover the bowl and put it in the fridge for anywhere from two to twelve hours before using. The trick is that there is something in the beer that eats up the ingredient in the flour which absorbs grease. The resulting mix will deep fry beautifully without absorbing any of the oil. The batter can be used to deep fry tomato slices, green peppers, onion rings, prawn and just generally anything that takes your fancy. I generally do my deep frying with the deep fryer set at 370°. I use the same temperature to do my potato chips which are just potatoes sliced into chip size, dried on a towel, and quickly deep fried. The batter seems to keep in the fridge for days and I can put the whole meal together in no time flat. The batter, of course, works equally well, if not better, on any type of cod.

If you are going to barbeque your salmon, I recommend that you brush each side of the portion lightly with oil and use a very low heat on the barbeque — about as low as you can get it. The real difficulty with using a barbeque is that the flesh tends to stick to the grill no matter how much it is greased and the low heat enables you to control this somewhat. The actual cooking time will depend upon the thickness of your portion, of course, and in each cooking operation the actual temperature of the fish when you start to cook is important. Barbeque time varies depending upon the type of barbeque so you will just have to keep checking the fish until it is just cooked, then serve it.

14

How To Build Your Own Rod

It is annoying to read the instructions in many "do-it-yourself" projects because of the complexity of the instructions and the unnecessary complexity of description surrounding even the most simple of assemblies. To build a fishing rod is truly a simple and satisfying task which will provide you with easy hours of interesting fun at little expense and will conclude with your being the owner of a first-class, custom-made rod as good as the best in any store and nearly as handsome. The assembly is so easy you will have difficulty believing what you are about to read. There are no tricks and nothing you can do short of attacking the glass rod with an axe or clamping it too tightly in the vice will mar the finished product.

The real impediment to the building of a glass rod is generally one's own lack of confidence. Like most things never done before, the idea of it is frightening. The nice part about building a rod is that if you make a mistake of some sort, the materials are so cheap, saving the blank, that you can scrap the mistake and start over.

The tools required are a couple of files and some emery cloth; everything else being generally at hand around home such as a razor blade and a pen to write your name on the rod, etc.

The first step is to buy a glass blank from your fishing tackle store which will probably have everything else you need except for the files and emery cloth. The choosing of the right blank can be done with the help of your tackle shop salesman. Choose a blank with lots of spine if you are building a mooching rod and the Fenwick 1262 blank mentioned earlier is a very good choice. It comes in two pieces with the ferrules already in place. Check to see that it joins together nicely with the ferules being true with the blank. Most rods have a "set" to them; that is they are made to be stiffer when being bent in one direction than they are on being bent in the opposite direction. This set or cast is generally indicated by a slight bend in the direction of the strength. The guide should therefore go on the opposite side of that, but it doesn't really matter. If you can't see the bend or set, don't worry about it.

The next step is to buy the handle corks which are small circles of cork about half an inch wide with a small hole through the center. You are going to have to calculate how long you want that rod handle to be and you can do that simply enough by looking at rods in the store and estimating the length if you haven't already measured one at home. An average mooching rod has about twenty-six inches of cork handle so you are going to need at least fifty-two corks and to be on the safe side, you will want a number of extras and of course some of them will be defective in any event. I generally buy seventy-five. You must at this time decide on the type of reel seat that you want. As you know there are the two types; one being firmly mounted on the rod and the other being a moveable type which slides on the corks. The fixed seat looks better, is firmer and holds the reel better, but you must remember that the sliding seat has the advantage of allowing you to place the reel exactly where you want and perhaps off-setting it a bit from the line of the guides. If your own rod at home has a fixed seat and you are happy with it, then buy one for the rod that you are building.

You will need to buy a butt-box which is the cap or end for the handle butt. They often have a rubber ball or circle at the end. Choose one that will not interfere with your rod holder and that is small enough to slip in and out of your rod holder with ease. At the time that you buy this butt-box, ask the man for a two-foot piece of butt-box twine which is a flat sort of thread used to assist in mounting the butt-box.

You will need a stick of ferrule cement to put the rod tip in place. By the way, after you have done this you should keep that stick of cement in your tackle box because it can sure come in handy when somebody's rod tip comes off. I generally keep a spare rod tip guide in my tackle box sufficiently big to slip over the end of almost anybody's rod in case of an emergency.

You have to choose the guides for your rod and here again, buy quality stock. These must be sturdy. Make sure that the weld or soldering union holding the little circle to the mounting bars is a good solid weld. Don't be shy about twisting the guide to make sure that this weld is done properly. In the old days you had to worry about the line wearing through the guides but most guides nowadays are made of carbide steel or have a sufficiently high carbon content to resist wear. Some guides have porcelain or glass inserts in them, but these are expensive and they also have a tendency to crack. They are, however, very beautiful and they make for a smart-looking rod. If you take good care of your rod you needn't worry about the cracking but on a boat rods are often abused inadvertently. The salesman will pick you out enough guides to adequately cover the rod that you are buying, but if either of you have any doubt, go find a rod on the rack of the same length as the blank you are using and count the number of guides. You might want to put an extra guide on to make the rod look a little better or you might want to put on one less. When you are buying the rod tip, make absolutely sure that it is of carborundum composition because that is the one guide that really has to withstand heavy wear. The clerk will choose one for you that slides over the glass blank top snugly after allowing for the ferrule cement. The ferrule cement is applied by heating it and it goes on somewhat thickly so there has to be room between the guide and the glass blank for the cement.

The nylon binding thread for the guides comes in many colors including thread of alternating colors. You must decide what color or colors blend best with your blank and remember that no matter which color it is, it is going to darken after you put varnish on it. You can choose a somber, plain color to give the rod a quiet classy appearance or you can dress it up with bright colors. There are silver and gold tapes that can be purchased which can be placed on the rod under the binding and this often gives it quite a smart look. Again, take a look at one of the rods in the store and see how that tape is used. Don't concern yourself with how complicated it looks — the use of the tape and putting the thread over it is a very simple procedure. I have always favored silver or gold tape on the little binding just before the rod tip because I like to have something bright up at the tip of the rod just to attract my eye if there is any action.

The thread comes in various calibres, from very fine to coarse. For your first rod and indeed, for most big rods such as a mooching rod, I favor the coarse thread for strength and utility.

To help preserve the color of the thread before you varnish it you will need a bottle of color preservative which is simply a lacquer you apply before varnishing the binding. Varnish that is applied directly to the bindings turns them very dark so that the color is lost and by applying a couple of coats of color preservative, the natural bright color of the thread is basically retained although the varnish still darkens it to some degree. Choose an expensive rod varnish if you have a choice because the one bottle will do several sets of bindings. You will need a small artist's brush and a little turpentine or substitute.

I forgot to tell you that after you have chosen the type of reel mount that you have in mind, be sure to ask if it will fit the type of reel that you have and if either you or the clerk is in any doubt, then have him take one of his reels out of stock and run a check on it. I remember one of the first rods that I did involved a fixed reel seat and when I had it all finished, I found that the seat wouldn't hold my reel. The air was sure blue, let me tell you.

The last of the items that you will need is the little hook-holding device which is an inverted wire "U" just where the handle corks end to enable you to insert your hook for carrying purposes. On a mooching rod the leader is very often too long for you to use this little hook and most moochers catch their hooks on the reel seat bar or onto the reel line-guide bar but this little device looks professional and you may want it. Under no circumstances should you ever imbed your hooks into your handle corks as this will ruin a rod handle very quickly.

You are probably going to have to go to your local hardware store at this point because the next items are not generally stocked in a sporting goods store.

If you have chosen the fixed reel mount, you will need to buy a roll of ordinary masking tape three-quarters of an inch wide. The accepted method of mounting your reel seat is to wrap the bare glass with this tape in a single width at each end of the space to be occupied by the reel seat. Then you slide the body of the seat, which should fit snugly, over the tape after having applied a little waterproof glue. This method holds the seat perfectly firm and avoids your having to make a wooden plug or dowel. I will explain exactly how to do this in a moment.

You will need a rat-tail file or two of them of different sizes to enlarge the little hole in the corks so that they will slide down the glass bank to fit snugly at the butt end where they belong. I generally use two, one small one to enlarge the small cork hole then a larger, coarse one to really take away the cork so that I can slide it down the rod. The large second rasp makes it easier to keep the hole truly round. You should be sure that these rat-tail files are coarse because it can be a slow process if you have picked too fine a file. A good idea is to try the rasp right in the hardware store on one of your corks. Remember that you have fifty corks to do and you want a file that really works.

You will need a coarse flat rasp for filing the outside of the cork handle to bring it down to size. You will need some emery cloth, not emery paper. You should have two weights of this emery cloth — one very coarse and the other very fine. Do not buy the little small squares in a package. Buy the big squares so that you can tear it and have a nice long piece to work with. Cork cuts very easily when you use emery cloth and you will only need a couple of sheets of each.

You need a tube of glue and I recommend LePage's Bondfast because it is an extremely good glue. The use of the epoxy glues is not necessary and if you make a mistake in putting on the corks, it is very difficult to remove the epoxy glue.

Now comes the fun. The first step is to do the handle. Use the rat-tail files to hollow out the corks one at a time. As each cork is done, slide it down the blank from the ferrule end. The blank is tapered so the first cork will have to have the biggest hole. The first three corks have to be fairly carefully fitted because they will later be sanded down almost paper-thin to receive your butt-box. If you are a confident sort of person, you can glue the corks into position as you hollow them out and in fact most people do it that way. For your first rod you might want to just slide them down and not glue them in place. You keep sliding corks down, gluing the corks to the glass with a little dab of glue and a little dab on the side of the cork to glue it to the one that is already on. You don't need to put glue all over both sides of the cork nor do you need to put glue all the way around the hole in the middle of the cork. Just a spot will do it. You must slide down enough corks to make the handle from the butt down to where the fixed reel seat is going to be mounted.

The next step is to mount the reel-seat tube on the glass blank. This is done by wrapping the masking tape neatly around the rod blank until your reel-seat tube fits over it snugly remembering that you want some glue between the tape and your reel-seat tube. Measure where you will need the second wrapping of masking tape and put that on then slide the reel-seat tube into position. You don't have to worry about which way it faces because the butt end of the rod doesn't have any "set" to it and it really doesn't matter which end is up. Apply generous glue to the masking tape, all surfaces, and to the inside of the reel-seat tube and then slide the reel-seat tube into position. At this point you had better take a break because you don't want to be doing too much work on the rod and disturbing the proper setting of the glue. You have probably done enough for the evening in any event so just leave it to dry firmly in position. You also want those three end corks dried firmly in position before you start working on the butt-box. I generally leave everything overnight before taking the next step.

The trickiest part of any rod handle is the mounting of the butt-box, so at this point I generally get out my heavy flat rasp and emery cloth and proceed to completely finish that first little section of cork handle because if anything is going to go wrong with the mounting of the butt-box, you don't want to have to remove the whole handle.

The one thing that will ruin a glass blank is to clamp it in a steel vice. Any pressure from steel jaws will crush the glass and so unless you are a handy man and can make some sort of a rod holder that won't crush the glass, the best thing to do is to have a friend hold the rod while you work on it or hold it yourself with one hand and work with the other. You can pad the vice jaws heavily with cloth and squeeze the vice only gently, but preferably it should be held in the hand for the next step which is to shape the corks to receive the butt-box. Use the rasp to bring them down to size. Leave lots of extra cork because you are going to want to sand it with the emery cloth and that emery cloth really does take that cork down.

You can ensure that the corks come out nice and round by holding your emery cloth as though you were going to polish your shoes with it and whipping it back and forth over the cork. This requires that someone hold the rod blank for you. Remember that coarse emery cloth really cuts quickly, so don't be too zealous; proceed slowly. Besides, you are supposed to be enjoying this. Sand the butt section down so that it receives the butt-box nicely using the fine emery cloth for the last bit. You should be trying the butt-box on the corks from time to time as you sand.

Don't worry about ruining it because you can still save the day by sliding new corks into place from the wrong end. They won't fit quite as nicely as sliding them from the other end, but they will still be acceptable.

Most professionals use butt-box twine which is wrapped around the last few corks to compress them just before you slide the butt-box on for the last time. You tie it so that it stays in place and it does make mounting of the butt-box considerably easier. You must smear the twine and the corks with glue and force the butt-box into position. It really looks sharp once it is in place. Allow this to dry overnight before you do anything else as you will probably knock it off if you try to continue with the rest of the corks.

Take a look at your finished product at this point and if you are not entirely satisfied with it, then simply take it all off and start again. There is no sense going on from this point if your butt-box is mounted at an angle or if it isn't strong or if there are holes in the cork or any other serious defects.

You are now ready to do the rest of the corks to complete the handle and so you go back to hollowing out the inside part and sliding them down the rod to meet the already-mounted reel seat and gluing each one into position.

If you have decided to use a sliding reel seat which fits over everything, then of course you have simply to start sliding the corks down the blank, making sure that each one is a fairly snug fit and either gluing them as you go or gluing them later. Remember not to glue on all of the corks if you are using the sliding reel-seat because you have to make sure that the sliding reel-seat doesn't come off the cork handle. You therefore have to slide it over the corks that you have on and then after having it in place, you add the last eight or nine corks.

To do this you stop about ten corks short of the full length of the handle. You will now rasp and sand the corks down as hereafter explained to where they just accept the sliding reel-seat and you will then add the last seven or eight corks, rasping and sanding them down to where they look acceptable but are still too big to allow the sliding reel-seat to slide off. Similarly, at the other end, the butt-box end, you will allow the corks to increase in size so the reel-seat won't slide off the butt end. The handle will then consist of a long, perfectly uniform area with slight rises at each end to prevent the reel-seat from coming off.

To fit the sliding reel-seat properly, you take your rasp or heavy file and start working on the handle corks with the seven or eight corks still remaining to be slid on from the ferrule end. By sliding the reel-seat down the rod blank you will have a rough idea just how small the handle has to be. Don't take too much off with the rasp. Try to avoid flat spots and remember that the tendency will be to take too much off the middle corks thereby making that part too small; you want that reel-seat on firmly. The best system is to start on the corks nearest the ferrule remembering that you mustn't take too much off with the rasp; coarse emery cuts quickly and you still have to use the fine emery. If you do start at the corks nearest the ferrule as suggested, but take too much off, it is a simple matter to cut off the ruined corks and slide a few more on and take another run at it.

The best system is to take the whole handle down until it is fairly round but still too big to accept the sliding reel seat. Then start to work on the end few corks, the ones nearest the ferrule, until they just accept the sliding reel-seat. Continue to work on them pushing the sliding reel-seat down each time you take a little more off. The sliding reel-seat has to slide down almost to the other end save for a distance of three or four inches which should gradually slope up to a point about a quarter inch from the butt-box.

This reel-seat should fit so snugly that you have to work it a little in order to slide it down the handle. Having completed this part of things you can try your reel on it to see if it fits before you put the last few corks in place. Don't snug the seat right down because this dents the corks. Just try it out gently until you know where it is going. If it doesn't work, or is unsatisfactory, return it for one that does work. The next step is to add the remaining corks and rasp and sand them to match what you have already done, but keeping them a little bit larger, of course, to prevent the seat from sliding off. The last cork is rounded slightly to give it a shoulder or if you are skillful you can put a bit of a "button" on it for better gripping.

Should you have elected to leave the corks unglued through all these operations, save of course for the three butt-box corks which must be glued before you can work on them, there is something you must do before you remove them for gluing and this is to run a good solid dark pencil line down the length of the cork you are going to remove for gluing because the corks have to be in line when you return them or else they will be out of round. The first time I did it we let the cork slide off onto the floor and it was almost impossible to put them back on in the right order.

The best system is to tie a rag around the rod down near the ferrule to prevent them from falling off. Then make your pencil line and slide the corks down, returning each one to its place with a drop of glue or two and lining up the pencil line. A touch of the emery cloth will remove the pencil line.

If you make a mess of the handle, but feel it is good enough, don't fool yourself. Take all the corks off and start again. You will not be happy with a second-rate product. This is a hobby to be worked on slowly over the winter nights, in your own sweet time, at your own pace and to be completed to your satisfaction. For what the corks cost, it just isn't worth not making the job perfect and something that you can be proud of. You are opening up a whole new field of fun for yourself and it is something that you can pass on to your children if they are interested. In the years to come you can repair all your own rods in professional style. It is not going to be any fun to show your custom-made rod to somebody if the job is shabby.

You are now ready to bind on your guides. The spacing is obtained by taking the measurements from one of your other rods or else take the measurements from one in a store or you can simply "wing it," taping each guide in place with one piece of masking tape or scotch tape and moving them here and there until they look right. A mooching rod has the guides all pretty much the same size or just getting a little smaller as they approach the tip. A spinning rod has a very large first guide being the one closest to the handle because it has to accommodate the whirling line.

Most mooching rods have just one guide on the butt blank but the odd one has two. Again you should look at one in the store to decide what you want. I favor just the one guide on the ten-foot blank, but I like to have two on the ten-foot-ten blank. Remember now that you have to measure exactly from where the reel is going to be mounted to the first guide making it an even three feet or an even arm's pull from the reel. It has to be a distance that you can use as a measure when you are stripping off your line. A smaller person may tend to favor even a two-foot distance. I think probably the best idea is to hold the rod in your right hand across your body as you now know how to do and just pretend that you are stripping off line and mount the guide four or five inches further than your hand. This is, after all, the distance that you will be working with and you will know that it is approximately three or four feet.

Having ascertained where you are going to mount the first guide, line it up with your fixed reel seat so that it will be in line with the reel and tape it to the rod with scotch tape or masking tape.

The actual binding is fun. You should wash your hands because you will stain the thread if you have grease or anything on your hands. First cut off a piece of thread about three or four inches long which you will use later to pull the end of the thread back under your binding. To start the binding, simply lie the thread on the rod making a circle around the rod and lie the thread over the end that you are burying.

The idea is to wrap over top of the end of the thread so that that end is held in place by the binding. Leave lots of tail so that it stays in place until you have started the binding and after about ten wraps over it, you can cut it off neatly with a razor blade. You should start the binding about an eighth of an inch from the end of the tang on a bigger guide and even more than that if you are planning on using gold or silver tape. The use of this tape will be covered later. After you secure the end of the thread under the binding then just slowly turn the rod, feeding the thread on strand against strand as you work your way along.

Don't worry about the odd gap in the thread because you can close those by pushing with your thumb. When you come to the guide tang, just keep going and the thread should bump up over that tang as you wrap up towards the guide which is held fast by the tape. You can adjust the width of that part of the binding which is not covering the tang by moving the guide a little as the tape will give and that is why it is not too critical where you start the binding. If the guide is a little warped so that the tang doesn't lie flat on the rod, you are going to either have to tape it down with a narrow piece of tape or else straighten it out with pliers. It is wise, of course, to check this before you start the binding because it is annoying to find that you have to stop halfway through the binding to fix the guide tang.

When you are a little past halfway along the tang with your binding, take the three-inch piece of thread that you had previously cut off and form a loop with it. Then lie the loop on the rod so that you can bid over it. The loop faces towards the guide and the tail simply lies along the rod because you are binding over it. You will use this loop to pull the end of the thread back under the last quarter inch of the binding so it is held there by the binding.

Make the binding come as close to the guide as you can. Now cut the binding thread free from the spool leaving only a short tail. Put this tail through the now-buried binding loop; you then pull the loop to draw the tail under the binding. You keep pulling it until the tail comes through the binding. You then throw the loop away and carefully cut off the thread tail with a razor blade where it comes out from under the binding.

The result is that both ends of the thread are buried under the binding. You will probably have ruined the first one, but do not be too quick to discard it. By the time you have two coats of color preservative and seven coats of varnish on it you will not be able to see too many of the little imperfections.

The masking tape is then removed from the other tang and you start over on that end. Remember to check the tang to see that it is lying flat against the rod. If not, tape it down with a narrow width of tape which you can rip off after you hae taken your binding up over the tang.

Remember to match the binding with the other side so that there is an equal amount of the binding lying on the rod before you get to the tang. The binding will slide on the rod a little when you first start, so you can adjust it some before you have too many wraps on the rod.

Some people use a book to run the thread through as they turn the rod to give them a little tension, but most find that the fingers feed the thread on just as well. If a binding turns out poorly, just cut it off and start again because, of course, you want to be happy with it.

You should do a binding up near the ferrule just for decoration and similarly you should do a binding running from the cork handle out for about half or even three-quarters of an inch. This is where you should put the little "U" to hold your hooks if you want to mount that device. You slide one end of the tang under the cork with a little glue on it and you bind the other end flat against the rod blank with your binding. If you wish, and I think it's a good idea, you should put a very narrow binding or even two of them about two inches down from this three-quarter inch binding which will create a space in which you can put your name or your name and your address. You can use India ink or a little white paint and the lettering is done with a pen. It takes but a moment or two to put it on correctly, but then you have to let it dry overnight before you apply some varnish to cover it. Having your own name on your rod is a nice touch.

You are now ready to put the guides on the tip section, remembering to place them on the opposite side of the "cast" or spine.

You should remember to do your binding when you are relaxed and not tired or cranky. As the guides get smaller, the bindng goes more quickly and is easier to do.

Installing the rod tip is easy, but you must remember one thing and that is that the glass tip is very susceptible to flame. You must not apply flame directly to the glass or you will weaken it. You should take the ferrule cement and, using a match, melt it and then smear a little of it on the tip while it is still in liquid form.

Now take a pair of pliers and, holding the tip in the pliers, heat the tip until it is good and hot - hot enough to melt the cement that you have smeared on the rod tip; then force the heated rod tip over the end of the rod, rotating it to make sure there is lots of contact with the cement.

You may have to take a couple of tries before the tip sets nicely, but don't be afraid to do this. The thing to remember is that you have to melt that resin that is on the end of the rod tip. Once the tip is in place and the ferrule cement dry, it is a simple matter to chip off the excess resin. You should now put a nice little binding up to the shoulder of that tip guide.

To use the silver or gold tape you simply place it on the rod just before the tang of the guide. Start your binding about an eight of an inch before the tape just as you would if the tape were not there. Bury the end of your thread as you do with any binding but then when you get up to the tape, you wind your thread over it with a gap between the turns so that the tape shows through. When you have covered the tape — it will take about three wraps — then just go back to your normal binding and the first thing you will be doing is to go up and over the tang. The effect is a little gaudy, but it does make a nice fancy binding.

The next step is to apply the color preservative to the bindings. Read the directions - it is very simple to use. The next step is the rod varnish and here again the directions on the bottle will carry you through, but do make sure you work in a quiet place where there is no air movement because dust on that varnish makes it look rough. I always put on seven coats of varnish but three coats is acceptable

You can use the color preservative on the area where you have put your name, being careful to apply it quickly with one stroke and only after the India ink or white paint has dried thoroughly. After that color preservative dries over the name, you needn't worry about it any more and that area gets seven coats of varnish also.

Do not varnish anything except the bindings; no matter how good the varnish, it will flake off the rod part in a few years due to the flexing. When I re-do my "store-bought" rods, I generally strip off all the old varnish and I leave it off, varnishing only the new bindings. It means the rod has rather a dull appearance but I find that more attractive than many coats of peeling varnish.

The only real danger area in the whole process is if you decide to clamp the rod in the vice. This can, and indeed usually does, damage the glass. You won't necessarily be able to see it but some day your rod will snap for no apparent reason where it was held in the vice. Similarly, if you have used your cigarette lighter on the rod tip to melt the ferrule cement, that will also snap off.

Your new skill will enable you to repair any rod at any time as well as providing you with a new rod each season should you decide to experiment or simply to add to your collection.